In the Land of Nyx

John Bowers

In the Land of Nyx

NIGHT AND ITS INHABITANTS

ANCHOR PRESS/DOUBLEDAY
GARDEN CITY, NEW YORK
1984

ISBN: 0-385-19196-D
Copyright © 1984 by John Bowers
All Rights Reserved
Printed in the United States of America
First Edition

Library of Congress Cataloging in Publication Data

Bower, John, 1928–
    In the land of Nyx.

    1. Bowers, John, 1928–   —Biography. 2. Authors,
American—20th century—Biography.   3. Night. I. Title.
PS3552.0873Z466   1984   813′.54[B]   83–14061

FOR LIS, NICHOLAS AND DAVID

In the real dark night of the soul it is always three o'clock in the morning.

F. SCOTT FITZGERALD

Hear that lonesome whippoorwill
　　he sounds too blue to fly

The midnight train is whining low
　　I'm so lonesome I could cry

I've never seen a night so long
　　when time was crawling by

The moon just went behind a cloud
　　to hide its face and cry.

"I'm So Lonesome I Could Cry"
HANK WILLIAMS

In the Land of Nyx

One

THE COTTON PRINT CURTAINS are drawn, but still that purplish haze penetrates. It comes from a neon light over some plants in the window directly across an air shaft from us. When Lis was pregnant and we first moved here, she thought that those rays did us harm, and she spoke nicely to Henry Geldzahler, the owner of the building next door, about it. Henry Geldzahler is a thoroughly nice man and must have solved some doozies as a renowned administrator in the art world. He had a cream-colored minishade installed between the neon and us. The light changed from ultramarine into a faint but persistent metallic glow. At 3:04 A.M. (as shown emphatically on the digital bedside clock, likewise glowing) I acknowledge the shade from Geldzahler's with a half-opened eye. I don't mind it so much anymore. It's part of home.

In the apartment above, a piano plays. I am told that this is jazz. It comes from the fingers of Peter, who has (on his own testimony) the night habits of a jazz musician but who makes his living as a judge for environmental matters in New York and as a referee of basketball games. The only tune I have ever been able to recognize from above has been the theme music from *Barry Lyndon*. I have caught myself humming that music more than once through the day. At first we also complained to Peter about the riffs which penetrated our ceiling and filled our space through the night. He was terribly chagrined that the sound had impinged on us, saying, "I'm so sorry. Really, my gosh, gee, I didn't realize." As a test he came down in the late afternoon and listened while a friend struck chords above. "My gosh, really, how loud that is," he said, sympathizing. A week went by with what seemed nervous pacing from above. Then slowly and inevitably the riffs crept back. At first only a few chords slipped in, then longer and longer segments—until it was as before. We beat it back to nothing a couple of times with complaints, to keep our hands in, and then bowed to fate and learned to live with it. I seem to recognize "April in Paris," or is that "Melancholy Baby"?

I close my eyes and scrunch into a fetal position. "No, no, NO!" from the bottom bunk bed in the kids' room across the hall. David is going through the Terrible Twos and is even saying "No" in his sleep. This wakes Nick in the top bunk. He screams. "Shut up down there! You doodie head!"

Lis pops up with a start. "What was that? What happened, what happened!"

"Nothing. One of the kids. Shssss. Let's see if they go back to sleep."

The elevator creaks outside. Pigeons coo. I pull an old blanket we inherited from Tennessee (a horse blanket, we suspect) over my shoulder and turn. My blue cotton pajamas—made in mainland China and for someone one foot shorter—creep up my back. I try an old method that I have periodically used since teenage days, gleaned from a long-forgotten source—a self-help book, a magazine article, health tips from high school? It entered my repertoire during a pubescent stage when I couldn't sleep, shortly after the time I stopped praying "Now I lay me down to sleep" and had lost my Baptist religion. I concentrate on my toes, totally relaxing them, then my feet, up my ankles and still coming until I get to my head, totally sagging. I let my mouth fall open. Who am I kidding? A whine, a low animal moan, breaks from above. It sounds like a wolf on the prairie. It is Ollie, a black and white spaniel, left alone. I flip over on my back. I think.

There is rent . . . five sixty-something . . . utilities—forty dollars, a hundred dollars—haven't paid phone for last two months . . . all that Master, Visa, American Express, Bloomie's, Macy's, Altman's, the garage, the ten-year-old car. . . . The phone company for some unfathomable reason is most cordial. Months can go by with unpaid bills before minor irritation shows. Worse is American Express, which sends telegrams and threats at the first sign of weakness on your part. Master

Charge and Visa get sneaky—slipping in interest costs and kiting the bill under a flurry of unasked-for brochures for luggage, cologne and commemorative silver disks. Con Ed is gracious and thanks one most kindly when bills are met on time. Go a little overdue and they turn waspish and lose those fine manners. In the space of twenty-eight days. The pit is a collection agency operating from some camouflaged locale—a P.O. box and phone number—given their head by some hospital charge gone astray or a whimsical shopper who ran up a tab in your name on a shopping spree in Tennessee. Those agencies and their devices can push you over the brink.

Oh, God, doctors and a hospital still hounding me, laboratory fees, sweet-natured dentists. . . . Lest we forget, Christmas gifts to super and his gang of help. . . . Moola required on the cabin upstate. . . . Rent the goddamn cabin, maybe, taxes to be paid up there and oil and plumbing repairs and roof practically coming down on our heads. . . . Can't lose cabin! . . . Kill me. . . . Kids need clothes and shoes. . . . Oh, sweet Jesus, I forgot school tuition! . . .

I see the onslaught of bills as a Black Glob of definite dimensions. It stands out there in space around the first of the coming month like Darth Vader. I am looking for another glob to cover it. It's like working with one of my kid's toys, fitting solid object onto solid object. Doing it while under water.

Teaching one college course, two sixty-something every two weeks. (Vision of two weeks like a blacktopped road with a fence on either side.) A black and lavender check coming in, pocket money only. . . . Novel not sold yet although it won three thousand dollars in a state grant on first forty pages. (Vision of four hundred sixty typewritten pages, triple spaced.) . . . Put guts into it, knew those characters, got them down, it's a true book, goddamnit, true, funny and alive and meaningful as I know life. . . . "Strawberry" Venable, I wonder where you are today. Back in Johnson City you reached adolescence before any of us. Nipples colored and puffed, dong down to knee. Brave and sophisticated enough to peep in girls' windows at night while they undressed. Ran track and shot pool—inside pants and in pool hall. Smoked. We used to think that getting hairs and having a large pecker and getting it in a woman were the most important things in the world. Maybe they are. . . .

Back in Johnson City the boys I once knew, ranks depleted, are now graying and aging. They live in colonials and split-levels and present pained, slow smiles to the world. They bring out Polaroid snaps of children. Some limp and show scars or travel in wheelchairs. . . . Life rolls mercilessly on, one moment a lad in a maroon and gold school jacket peeking in girls' windows, the next a tired, slump-shouldered dignitary in polyester. Is "Strawberry" himself someplace now, rocking away, thinking of me, thinking of how he used to be able to beat the shit out of me (and everyone else) at will? . . . A few are picked out—by whom?—to be psychiatrists and bankers and lawyer-politicians; others haunt the poolroom until it's leveled and still live with their mothers and lose their teeth and hair and marbles. . . . And inside each is that boy who once climbed those long steps to Science Hill High on a sunny spring morning, the grass so green back then, the sky so blue. . . . Oh, me. . . . Life moves on in New York as well . . . scything heads off, moving someone to Beekman Place on a roll of the dice, another to the Bowery, as if in a for-real Monopoly game. . . . Some lie broken and discarded. . . . Others do exercises upside down on a chinning bar and have their faces lifted and give credit for their worldly success to hard work. . . .

Mario has pulled down 2.5 million on a book he hasn't even written yet, for God's sake. . . . Mario in tight black overcoat, like Edward G. Robinson, plug of cotton in his ear because of an infection, when we both worked side by side at Magazine Management. Couldn't pay the docs. Home almost foreclosed on him before *The Godfather* stayed the sheriff. Good old Mario. He deserves it. I could shoot him. . . . Everybody hits him for a loan now. He throws fins and sawbucks around like confetti. I remember when they turned him down at *Playboy* and *Esquire* and sank *The Fortunate Pilgrim,* such a wonderful book. . . . Tom Wolfe owns a town house. So does Robert Gottlieb. I saw a man the other day who used to be a star reporter at the New York *Post.* Drunken, battered face, poor fucker, in cotton clothing in the freezing rain. . . . Remember a man who was the spitting image of Tom Wolfe in jail in Elizabethton, Tennessee.

Even talked like him, soft and gentle-like. Wonder what put
Tom in an East Side town house and his double in the jug? What
brought me from the early morning dew of Tennessee to the
jangle of New York?

Vision of the Black Glob. Oh, how am I going to cover it!

Teaching. We've counted that already, bozo. *Cosmo.* Must
finish that assignment. "Men in Bed." (An involuntary moan
from me, counterpunched by Ollie's from above.) Good wife
touches my hand in comfort in her sleep. Ollie has nobody. Let's
see. . . . Five pages a day. Twenty by the weekend—enough
for the bloody thing. Helen will want insertions. Is it because
Cosmo is a female organ? Insertions, always insertions. What
was it the long-gone cynical managing editor said about *Cosmo?*
"We offer shopgirls a little diversion on the way to the grave."
. . . OK, we'll ask for half the money before insertions. I'll go to
Hearst bookkeeping in their dreary bookkeeping building and
get it. Deposit it. Pay rent, tuition, stiff hospital, the docs, pay
the stores, minimum to the cards. . . . Let's see. . . . All this
trouble getting money out of *Cosmo* and last summer their
machines or brains went haywire and they sent me two thousand dollars out of the blue. Two thousand smackeroos. For
nothing. The system just went berserk for one beautiful moment. But so many bills and checks were coming and going that
I didn't even notice. Thought it was something they owed me
until they caught the error. The money itself evaporated like
smoke up the flue. They thought, I knew, that I'd cashed it like a
criminal. I feel like a criminal, too, guilty to the core. . . . Got
to pay that two grand back somehow. Someday when I'm old
and gray, lady. I can't even cover the Black Glob for the coming
month. . . .

> Darliiiiing, I am growing olllllllld.
> Silver threads among the gollllllld . . .

Above—*yowlllllll!*

Wonder who's out there not thrashing about and worrying,
someone sleeping like a baby? I would pick someone in Oyster
Bay, someone with a couple of limos in the garage, a couple of
million in blue-chip stocks, a tennis court and a Jacuzzi. How
could those people have a care? . . . They do—somehow,

someway, no matter the gravy train they board. They want a little more, or their own wondrous world turns in on them. Klaus von Bülow . . . how were you getting through the nights up there in Newport, your wife a vegetable, millions an inch from your fingertips, the gumshoes breathing on your neck? You had your worries, I know. . . .

And Philip Hehmeyer, erstwhile head of the Cotton Exchange, thirty-seven, gentleman, bachelor, good-looking, East Side swinger, took a shotgun to himself and left this world. . . . Hehmeyer, originally of Memphis, Tennessee, a University of the South at Sewanee grad, seemed in my books to have it made. Lord, he was even president of Sigma Alpha Epsilon at Sewanee. Remember the rarefied air members of SAE walked through at the University of Tennessee? The very bricks of their smart corner house in Knoxville oozed elegance and aplomb. The ATO house across the street (where I was entombed) seemed dark and forbidding and a retreat for those who were out of it. How blond and troubleless and moneyed those SAE-ers back in Knoxville had seemed. Even now, decades later, I sometimes dream of that SAE house across the street where refinement, exclusiveness and the good times rolled, all in elegance. Note, too, that SAE-ers got the girls. Their legend of money in the pocket and their elitism carried the day. I felt none of them could possibly be unhappy. And now, Philip Hehmeyer, SAE, does himself in in New York City.

Someone sneezes, the blast carried by the air shaft out our window. God bless you. A man-woman fight goes on in the far distance. Its clamor is so distant that it has the tinny reality of a radio station caught on a barely audible rim. Somewhere, though, the fight must really be shaking the dust. My old fights and concerns flicker on the periphery of the mind like this fight. Close up, when they were happening, they were consuming and awesome—now they slide in and out of memory with a dim, dull ache. . . . Yet, give me half a chance, and I'm back there arguing with my old boss in Washington, D.C. I see his burr haircut and chubby cheeks, hear his goofy laugh and pious, second-rate opinions. Goddamn, decades later I'm still arguing with him. We did nothing there, no work, nothing. We fought office politics and lived in fear. That was it. He's telling me I'm sloughing off my duties and have a meager talent for drafting official correspondence. He's getting ready to hand over a Performance Rating, eyes lowered, head ducked, in his office with the door closed. I'm still answering him. "Look, what are you driving at?" I'm saying at three-something in the morning in New York, angry all over again. "You're the laziest son of a bitch I've ever encountered. Not only that but you're an idiot. All you do is make jokes about minorities and take endless coffee breaks. And for this you're a GS-14!"

I've talked to him for over two decades in these late stay-awake hours. I didn't say much of anything to him at the time. Took it. He was Boss. . . . Nor did I really let loose at Helene back then. She kept me on a string of my own choosing for an eternity. Was I out of my mind? Am I out of my mind now? Are there grown, responsible men now tossing about in the middle of the night, remembering an eighteen-year-old girl with a slightly pigeon-toed walk and big, weepy eyes? Is Henry Kissinger remembering a tootsie who once did him in? Is he carrying on a conversation with her—as I am with mine? "So, Helene," I say to her, as I never did at the time, "you've been seeing Pearson on the side. All the time I've been declaring my undying love, you've been tooling around with him. A guy who lives in my own rooming house. A guy I see every day. You did it. OK, fine. You've taught me that treachery extends to teenagery. I walk out, my dear. You will never see me again!" I see the way her hose drooped on her legs—never could get it held up. Never could get the simple task of a garter belt down pat. I see the brownish crack between her two front teeth (only she had it), hear the laugh with lips puckered to hide the gap (only she did it). I feel the warm Washington sun and the terror of being under constant surveillance in my piddling, useless job in a sensitive agency. God, were there ever ways to drive a sane man nuts in Washington, D.C.! My mind digs up a hundred snapshots, which are always on call in my brain—the narrow streets of Georgetown, the endless halls of the State Department, the white heat of summer. If I'd stayed back there and somehow married a Helene with drooping stockings, I'd be a GS-14 now. Hell, I'd be retired on a half pension. . . .

Wooo weee! James Joyce was a writer of the night—those

rambling night thoughts of good old Molly Bloom, the accidental, involuntary thought that bubbles up from Joyce. Poor bastard lived in penury, had to flee the debt collectors hither and yon in Europe. . . . Let's see, all of his work now in print and used as college texts, he'd have a nifty annual income if he were still trucking. He would be a hundred. Dead, no longer able to dream of sniffing ladies' drawers anymore. Gone. I remember back home in Tennessee, waiting for everybody to clear out, and then pulling *Ulysses* down from a high shelf, where it just naturally fell open to the soliloquy at the end. I could almost quote it. I couldn't believe it was in a book, between covers. Molly Bloom. She thought in words, not images—otherwise, Joyce couldn't have pulled it off. I see a curvy, long-haired woman stretched out in bed. Moonlight seeps in; she fidgets. The night is long.

Wonder if I could write at night? I'm up now. But I wasn't taught that way. I was taught to arise early, at first light, not say much, and then march like a robot to the typewriter. You would write in a calm, even way. By nighttime you were too stimulated, tired, emotional, crazed, drunk. There was no chance for a schedule. Another James—James Jones—used to snap to at dawn, swing wide his trailer door, hawk up phlegm, break mighty wind, and then sit down before his grand typewriting machine. I've followed his example ever since and still hear Lowney Handy's words in my ear: "Do it in the morning. Put it down cold." I've been brainwashed ever since. . . . And all this advice was directed to the Artist, not to a contributor to *Cosmo* and a cranker-out of girlie mag prose. It was for the Serious Writer. . . . I conjure up my finished work after all these years, after much water has flowed and poured over the dam. All this struggle and angst . . . for *this? Mamma mia*. . . .

Joe the Doorman shakes the trash out by the service elevator, rattles the service elevator door—I suspect to wake those within earshot. I think I hear him mumbling, but that would be impossible from the distance. It's just that I know he's always muttering and complaining. I am glad I do not have a laundry to pick up and Joe to chauffeur me down by elevator. Joe does not like night work. He will be philosophical—shrug and mutter, "What are you going to do? It's there. I gotta do it." But he does not like it. He works it to survive. It's murder to go down with him to the laundry room. He'll leave you stranded with an armload of hot bags while he disappears upward by elevator. You ring, you curse, you drop your bags to dirty cement and ring again. No Joe. He has the same lame excuse when finally he creaks open the ancient door, eyes sad and rheumy behind smudged glasses. "I had a party upstairs coming in from the country. Lots of people coming in from the country. They bring in all these things. . . ."

I never find out who all these people are who come in from the country and why it takes him so long to service them. I thought my own family was the only one trudging back and forth Okie-style between city and country. Maybe that's where Joe got the idea that such a doorman's nightmare exists. And he wants to pay me back for all the armloads of logs and wild-flowers and bikes he's been forced to unload from our vintage VW in the late evening hours. Or maybe he just wants to strike back at anyone and everyone (leave 'em cooling with their fuckin' laundry!) who has the nerve to snooze between sheets through the night. Joe does not take kindly to the night shift.

I remember my father. Not a day goes by I don't think of my father. Maybe it's a brief shot of his face at the family dinner table or his walking up the front steps swiftly or bringing a Coke to his lips at the newsstand downtown in Johnson City. But I think of him. I can now—tossing over, pulling the sheet as much over my head as possible and unfortunately off Lis—feel myself in his strong arms when I was six, Nick's age. He's holding me up, cradling me, and it's night and we're watching a house on fire on Boone Street Hill. I can see leaping sparks and charred smoke against a black sky. I hear the crackle, too, and see or-ange flames licking behind windows. I still smell the fire and feel the terror in the air. The place had been a neighbor's home up until a few minutes before. Now this family—not unlike our own—stood quietly and forlornly at the front of the crowd. I don't remember how I got there with my father, just that we were there. I still sense the security I felt in his arms. What would he say to this yard-long stack of bills coming in under the door (we have no mail box here)? What would he say to the fifteen hundred dollars owed to ordinary old Master Charge? He never owed anyone anything as far as I know. He eventually retreated from even having to owe anyone a hello. He took night work. He learned to dislike the day.

What were my father's worries? I'll never know exactly. He told jokes, took snoozes, and walked to town. He told me often that the Depression had been rough and that you had to make compromises in marriage and that was about it. He didn't have a chance for nighttime worry sweats, for he worked then, on call for trains hurtling through town. Did trouble make him thrash about in daytime? Did he awake at noon, say, and stare at the watermarked ceiling unable to fall back asleep? I think not. When I shook him awake in late afternoon—my first chore after coming home from school—he was sawing logs. So little I did know about my father in a fundamental way. He shined his own black shoes, wore socks that came over the calves and were held up by garters, and he wore abbreviated B.V.D.'s in summer and long johns with a flap in winter. He never complained—ever. He never had a headache, a bad cold, or felt out of sorts enough to mention it. He never said he had bad luck or blamed a misadventure on anyone else. He endured right through the railroad disappearing, my mother's fatal accident, the home sold and leveled and his moving into the Appalachian Christian Village, no alcohol allowed on premises and prayer before every meal.

He even endured a surgeon's knife in his mid-eighties, the grumpy wielder of the blade not finding the prostate in one entrance, slicing through in another, testy about answering any questions before and after. My father was sitting up in a chair, in his old red bathrobe (which I wear now), a very short time later. He looked at a loss at what had been inflicted upon him, a mute, questing, dazed look in his hazel eyes. He hurt. But he asked if everything was going all right with me, would I be able to make my plane flight on time. There was no night to crawl to now— except the final one. No railway station to retreat to and wait out the hours before dawn. He tried, in the hospital wing of the Appalachian Christian Village, to escape in a thin patient's gown out a narrow casement window. He was caught with a bare leg out of it—a nearly hairless old man's leg—and was thereafter tied when in the hospital bed by a kind of primitive harness. . . .

There are such terrible nights out there for some—far worse, I know, than mine tonight. But mine's all I got. . . . Someone's sweating out one or more of the five cancer signals. I keep my hand in there, too. I have a cough and I've seen blood through all orifices. And how about the wart or two and the mark that keeps darkening? No loss of weight, knock wood. And nothing's been excised. Think if you'd had an organ plucked out and were sweating out the five-year wait. Someone is mulling that over tonight. Somebody is dreaming up ways of killing Boss or Battleax, Lover or Friend. Who doesn't thrash about? Anyone? Maybe Reagan. He must sleep at night—else why do they have to wake him at three when a Brezhnev dies? Is Dick Nixon or George Steinbrenner hugging a pillow? Oh, Sidney Skolsky, where are you now? At the end of your columns you used to tell us how the Great Ones slept. Monroe sleeps between satin in the buff. . . . Somewhere in an otherwise sleepy little town a young man is certainly having the night sweats over the young woman who hasn't come around at the crucial time of month. Oh, I so know him! He sees himself enslaved for the rest of his life, sentenced to a breadwinner's role for eternity in a place where absolutely nothing happens, no chance at escape. He indeed has a reason to toss about. . . .

And the woman undoubtedly wonders if he's going away, abandoning her like a heartless cad. Somebody's embezzled a bundle. Someone's put the boots to a nubile thirteen-year-old and waits for the law to break down the door. Someone's sunk a fortune in a chicken farm. Someone bought an Edsel. Someone bought a color TV, a wardrobe, complete household furnishings and a washer/dryer courtesy the friendly E-Z Credit Corp., payments due to begin at the crack of dawn. It's the night after the party when you said that awfully crude thing to that nice woman with an instant flush to her cheeks, that woman who turns out to be the daughter or wife of the man you work for. . . .

Wonder how Updike sleeps and Joyce Carol Oates? Surely like babies, their typewriters still smoking in the corner. Philip Roth only has to worry about someone who took up most of an issue of a magazine to give him a lousy review. . . . I asked my students at the university the other day who had read Edmund Wilson (he was called "Bunny" by intimates, class). Not a hand went up. Who has heard of Edmund Wilson? Not a movement. Who has heard of Tom Wolfe the Second, the journalist, the one living today, not the novelist of the past. . . . No one. Here are seniors in an Eastern-seaboard college, most of them English majors. What chance do I stand? I saw a photo of Wolfe the other day in what looked like a snappy punting jacket, a dashing white border around the cloth (love to have one), in an ad for his latest collection. Ad took up a whole page in the Sunday supplement. Tom looks out in a jovial, confident way, a man in his beginning autumn years, a fox who's just been in the chicken coop, a man assured of his place in the literary kingdom. . . . Wolfe and I came to the city at the same time in our salad days, he to the *Herald-Trib,* me to wildly imaginative and unspeakable magazines. We actually left the same place behind (although not together)—Washington, D.C. . . . Oh, "Men in Bed" now for *Cosmo!* I've got to write it! Wouldn't it be nice to get lost at night for a while, like my father did at the railway station, to never have to make a daytime appointment, look at a daytime face, or hear daytime news?

But could your body take it? Bodies seem to take a battering on the night shift. Look at hookers and jazz musicians. There is a weary slump to the shoulders after a while. No one does a fast shuffle. Eyes ache and are brightly veined. Duke Ellington, the compleat night owl, had bags under his eyes that belong today in the Smithsonian, appendages the size of golf balls. Bad diets, bad sleep, smoky rooms and no one stopping you from the whims of dissipation. Of course, some people are strong enough to make night work for them, to adjust and not go off the deep end. My father was one. Sergeant Artie Cappabianca of the 13th Precinct here in Manhattan is another. Cappabianca keeps to a tight schedule, makes his hours regular under the circumstances, and keeps his health. He even wears a bulletproof vest which balloons out his jacket. His health comes first, but he likes the night differential pay. . . .

Then there is Lester, the Carnival Fixer in the South whom I knew. Day is lost for him, a blurry, fuzzy period. He wakes in late afternoon in whatever trailer or motel he has bedded down in the previous dawn. Sometimes it's his own trailer with wife and infant daughter. His face puffy, beard grizzly, eyes watery, he feels various pains most intently. He will watch a fly buzzing around a dead beer can from the night before. Watch it for minute after minute. Reminds him eventually to grab a fresh one from the refrigerator. I saw him originally in Lynchburg, Virginia, where his ragbag carnival was playing in a magnificent southern spring. I see him now in my mind. In a gray T-shirt, boxer shorts that could use washing, and feet in unlaced black shoes, he watches his baby in diapers crawl. He watches her abstractly, the way he watched the fly. He gets in a nagging, desultory disagreement with Kathy, his teenage wife—it has no force or ginger, more like the low-key rumblings of testy zoo simians than anything else. Lester scratches his hairy lump of a belly underneath his T-shirt and then shades his eyes. It is a young man's face. Somehow, with infinite pains, in slow motion, he dons pants from last night and a freshly ironed shirt from a drawer. He combs his curly blond hair and leaves glistening drops of water on it. He tells Kathy good-bye. Rather he mumbles something indistinct, the tone a farewell. She says nothing, cradling her now wailing baby in soiled diapers in her arms. She wears tight shorts, and she seems burdened and oppressed and resentful, but, despite it all, vaguely self-satisfied and pleased.

She had wandered on the midway in some small southern mountain town sometime before and met Lester the Fixer. She was from an enormous family, and she hadn't been more than fifty miles from home before. "She hadn't worn shoes," Lester told me. "I got her a color TV and give her a baby. What more could a woman want? She didn't know nothing before she tied up with me."

Lester is not a homebody. He drives his air-conditioned Cadillac to the motel restaurant where fellow carnies have gathered in early twilight. All are rousing themselves now as the sun throws late golden streaks through the windows. Lester begins to perk up. He eats a couple of soft-boiled eggs, his tribute to a diet. His belly is big and impossible to disguise, and Lester is conscious of appearance, not a little bit vain. He has more beer, and sweat breaks out on his upper lip. He begins talking, a monologue, which will continue through most of the night. The sun sets in golden needles as the fluorescence of the restaurant becomes stronger. Lester talks about what a great Fixer he is— the man who pays off the Law to be able to operate the clip joints, the man who soothes the hysterical marks who've been taken, the final one to make sure the machinery functions. "I'm the best, I'm the goddamnedest best in the business."

It's a ratty little carnival: a ferris wheel that tilts precariously, a slew of girlie shows at the far outer rim, and a line of gypsy and take-a-chance booths at front. The battered, listing merry-go-round pipes a chipper "Beer Barrel Polka" over and over into the air. Night has fallen. Bare electric light bulbs burn hotly in an arch at the entrance of this enterprise that bears no name— perhaps it never had one. A string of these unshaded white bulbs runs the oblong course around the midway. There is a soft scent of spring and budding plants beyond and damp and dirty sawdust beneath. It's tawdry and evil-seeming and richly menacing—and on every carny's face, in the man-made electric light, is a look of beatific expectation and complete aliveness. Those puffy hang-dog faces I'd seen in the motel's restaurant in late afternoon now glisten. They bark out their spiels, looking for the perennial hayseed and sucker. Lester the Fixer, filled to the top with beer, works the midway, solving problems, philosophizing, paying off and receiving kickbacks. (He got a cut every time a mark was taken.) This is nighttime in Lynchburg, Virginia, with a roving ragtag band of outlaws—and I stayed with them during their stop. I got to really know them. . . .

I see Lester now, taking a pee beside the office-trailer on the midway . . . I see a line of rubes snaking in a girlie show . . . I see the most innocent-looking girl, with dark bangs and red cheeks, a carny to the core, taking a mark at a ring toss game. . . . And I lie in a queen-sized bed in Manhattan and wonder what economic force has put the quietus on me, what scam has been perpetrated on my wallet, why am I sweating blood over moola at—let's see—four-eighteen in the morning?

It takes me a split second or two to cover the carnival terrain and its host of characters in my mind. A few battings of the eye: a deputy sheriff in pressed khakis and pinched smile, standing on a darkened hill and gazing down, as if on prey, at the lit carnival below; Jean the Stripper telling me she had met Dean Martin in Las Vegas; a dirty-faced gypsy trying to coax me into her mitt camp. . . . In fact, I can go over my whole life in about the time it takes to turn over in this bed, considering the tangled sheet I have to unravel and straightening the Chinese pajama bottoms which have a tendency to turn around the opposite way. . . . I replay the night before I entered North Side Grammar School in Johnson City, age six. It was the first night I remember not being able to sleep—and I experience once again the drama and anxiety. I couldn't wait! I was up at sunrise, running through the house. I still see the early sun outside the kitchen window as my mother sleepily makes breakfast. (The first boy I met in school, someone in overalls and cracked brown teeth, took me immediately into the bathroom and demonstrated how to smoke in a stall.) I whip out mental snapshots of halcyon days at North Side, on to junior high and senior high. Mooning over girls, worrying in bed . . . the people who have come and gone, their faces and moments with them. High school graduation night and the car wrecks which followed. . . . A troop train ride in Korea late at night. . . . Being a gambling shill at Lake Tahoe and watching a man have a heart attack at the blackjack table, the cords in his neck swelling to the size of tow ropes. (They laid him under a crap table until the medics arrived. Didn't want to disrupt play.) . . . Los Angeles, and driving a cab through fog in Santa Monica, miserable and lost. (I never could learn the city streets.) . . . James Jones in a silver trailer, and yearning to emulate him. . . . Washington, and living in fear and paranoia. . . . Exhausted in New York.

I see a number of people on the tree of night. Duke Ellington sits in great satisfaction on one branch. Up above him James T. Farrell is swinging at someone. Bradley Cunningham rests back against the trunk, smoking. . . . I have always been drawn to outcasts, and so many outcasts are drawn to the night. I have every characteristic of a night person—a distaste for bosses, a hatred of the expected, an obsession with gaining an ultimately nonexistent freedom—every quality except one. I can't stay awake after a while. I fall asleep.

Two

MY FATHER WAS Tip Richard (T.R.) Bowers and he worked nights. He worked as a telegrapher for the Southern Railway, a job about which he never had one good word to say. I remember going to his room on the second floor of the frame house at 203 West Watauga Avenue, Johnson City, Tennessee, to awaken him at around three in the afternoon. His pants lay by the iron frame bed, accordion-fashion, belt buckle flopping. The shades were drawn, slivers of afternoon light glowing along the edges. Traffic noises sounded from the street, which was a stretch of Highway 11-E. The room reeked of sleep—jumbled sheets, blanket musk, and an undefinable aroma of my father asleep. My father shaved and bathed in late afternoon and then ate his breakfast. A couple of hours later he ate another meal, because that was the time the rest of us ate supper and he wished to accommodate. From then until ten-thirty he whiled away time until he picked up his battered green lunch box with thermos of coffee, donned a gray felt hat in winter (a straw one in summer), kissed my mother, and took the fifteen-minute walk to the depot downtown. The rest of us went to bed a short time later. When I heard his soft tread on the porch at seven-thirty in the morning, I knew all was well and it was time to get up.

My father was six feet three and wore his gray hair in a pompadour, and was impossible to prod to anger except through three sources—the Southern Railway, the Republican Party, and the mischief of my older brother. Many times I burst into his room to wake him, caught up in events of the day and oblivious to my father's groggy, confused state. "I just made the basketball team, Dad!"

"Who's that? Who's that? . . . Oh, that's fine, son."

I never considered him broken from day's patterns, and disregarded the fact that he didn't tread through the noon's fierce light. I passed on information and sought fatherly advice and pride and consolation while his hands groped in the shaded room and his watery hazel eyes tried to focus on a form suddenly plopped on the edge of his bed. "Dad, Dad, look at *this!*"

It was a form letter with a crimson and white escutcheon at the top. Harvard had turned me down for admission. I didn't have the qualifications—certainly not the money—but I was applying to various revered seats of learning; all it took at that time was a three-cent stamp. I was so proud to have a letter from Harvard that it hadn't quite sunk in on me yet that they didn't want me there. The afternoon mail had just arrived, and I hadn't a second thought that I shouldn't rush to my father's room to let him see a communication from Harvard University. (My mother was running a bookstore downtown then, and it was just my father and me at home.) He rose on one elbow in his abbreviated B.V.D.'s that spring afternoon and tried to comprehend what this embossed page, ripped from an envelope, meant. "I can't see, son."

I raised the shade and handed him his glasses, and he finally said, after his eyes went over and over it, "Well, that's all right, son. I wouldn't worry about it."

My father grew up on a large farm, the youngest of twelve children. His father was a doctor (learning his trade as a physician's helper in the Civil War) and a farmer. When he died, the land was split up twelve ways. My father sold his share to pay for training as a telegrapher (a thriving profession, one that had claimed Andrew Carnegie among its ranks), and married my mother, a country schoolteacher. Until the Great Depression he not only worked as a telegrapher but sold insurance and managed a semiprofessional baseball team. He drove and owned a Chevrolet. He owned a house. When the Great Depression struck (coinciding with my birth), he lost his job. He never drove a car again. He had to move his family from the house he had bought and now had to sell, and set up housekeeping with my aunt and her son, pooling resources, as an accommodation to hard times. When the Southern Railway began rehiring, my father took night work. For the rest of his working life he worked nights. Even when he had seniority and could opt for day work, he chose night. He at first chose Second Trick, from three in the afternoon until eleven, which had a patina of light in its earlier hours to recommend it—then Third Trick, from eleven until seven in the morning, which, no matter the solstice or season, was nearly totally black. First Trick, in daylight, the most prized by other telegraphers, the one that seniority led to as a golden reward, a schedule that let you live like most of mankind, my father turned down. He wanted nights.

He became increasingly and quixotically deaf, and he said that the dark hours suited him better. My mother remembered a woman banging on the ticket counter in early evening at the depot, saying, "Ticket to Limestone! Ticket to Limestone!" My father, a step away, did not hear or chose not to hear this plea. A steady, secret fear in our family was that my father would one day miss an important clickety-click on the telegraph and let two trains collide. It never happened. His ear turned sharp at night for the strange clicks of the telegraph. He wore head-phones, a black clasp across his gray pompadour, steadily jig-gling messages by thumb and forefinger on the telegraph key. He moved trains around and sent and received signals from other stations. At first it was steam engines, then diesel, and when airlines began taking over, my father worked his last trick and retired. He had never taken a day's sick leave and during World War II had worked seven nights a week without one night off.

As a little boy I thought that only great and strong men worked at night. As a treat I got to take him his supper when he worked Second Trick. I carried an oval Christmas fruitcake tin that housed deviled eggs, hard-boiled eggs, fried-egg sand-wiches, biscuits and ham, and wedges of coconut cake. I particu-larly liked those deviled eggs my mother made and not infre-quently ate them on the way to the station. My father never complained. I also tightrope-walked the train tracks on the way, balancing the lunch tin on my head. Occasionally I lost my balance and the tin fell to the cinders, biscuits and eggs wrapped in paraffin paper tumbling out. I did the best I could to pick out the grit and scrape off the dirt. But I then couldn't help but watch in fascination as my father happened to discover a small rock between his teeth. He laughed about it a short time later, too.

During summer nights, when I was not in school, I stayed up with my father until Second Trick ended and sleepily rode his shoulders as we plowed home. I had gotten to type on his typewriter, banging out letters and getting him to read me what I had written. I watched him clicking messages out, saw a green button light flash on, and felt the first stirrings from the track that announced a steam-engine train approaching. I stood beside my father, a few feet from the track, holding one of his large hands, while he raised a message on a bamboo hoop with the other for an engineer to snag. The night had been filled with cricket noises outside the open depot windows, the crunch of feet on cinders, harsh strong light in the depot, darkness without. By the tracks one smelled the country night air of honeysuckle and dew-wet grass mixed with the scent of crosstie tar and oil drippings from trains. The depot burst with light through the night, like a grand ship on a dark sea amid dimly lit buoys. Life was being lived inside. Strong grown men—railroaders—had wrestled a space out of the dark, sleepy air. The railroaders who barged into the depot smiled easily, had their sleeves rolled up, and always had a word to say to me, especially about baseball and the cast of characters in the major leagues. It was impossible to believe the stories about some of these men. A Mr. Denton was a Section Boss—one who drove Section Hands to lay crossties and rip up rails. "He's a mean 'un. He can cuss a mile a minute. Section Hand don't carry his load, Denton'll floor him. Put him right out with a sock to the jaw. Damn man's crazy." Mr. Denton was the most gentle among them to me. He wanted to know where I fished and what vegetable I was responsible for in our garden (radishes), and he showed me magic tricks with a piece of string. He never got bored with me or told me he didn't have time to play. I asked him about his reputation for socking Section Hands and never losing a fight. "It's a job I got to do, son. Don't ever be a railroader."

These railroaders swaggered with a confident air, and they spit tobacco juice halfway across the depot into a lone, foul spittoon. They then tucked their lower lip over their upper one and wiped quickly with the back of their hand. They enjoyed

my father's company and found him funny and witty. I had
never thought of my father as particularly funny, but I took
their word for it. He would say a word or phrase that I didn't
understand, and these men would hee-haw and hold their sides.
My father never seemed sleepy during the late-night hours. As I
rode his shoulders going home from Second Trick, I tried to
keep the feeling of freedom and the sense of a party going. I
would bang the Christmas tin on my father's head to get some
reaction and he would gently admonish me. "Not so hard, son."
I tried to keep my eyes open going up Boone Street Hill, but the
rhythmic swaying on my father's shoulders and the late hour
often put me out. I seldom remembered being tucked in bed.

Sometime during World War II my father moved further into
the night, taking Third Trick. He hadn't made World War I and
now he was too old for World War II. He didn't take that much
interest in patriotism anyhow. Or religion. I remember walking
toward the depot with him when a troop train filled with brand-
new recruits was slowly winding its way through Johnson City
and headed for an induction base somewhere. "Hey, Four-F!"
one of the recruits, a half-pint of whiskey in his hand, called to
my father. "Why don't you join up, you Four-F fucking draft
dodger!" I pretended not to hear. I don't think my father could
actually hear. He walked straight on, only up a couple of hours
into the late afternoon and his face still slightly gray from sleep.

On Third Trick my father dealt only with the late-night pas-
senger and the hard-core owl. He swore he heard better in the
late night air when fewer sounds distracted him from what he
really wanted to hear. He laid claim to the davenport in the
living room from right after supper until he took his store-
bought lunch pail, which had replaced the old Christmas tin,
and marched off into the night at ten-thirty. He read Dickens,
front to back, from *Sketches by Boz* to *The Mystery of Edwin
Drood*, chuckling to himself and sometimes reading aloud. The
rest of us would take our eyes off of him for a moment, begin
talking, and frequently hear snores begin to cascade from the
davenport, full of whoops and whistles and lip flutters. We
thought nothing of it, talking a little louder to get over the
sounds. When a visitor's tread sounded on the porch we shook
my father awake in a show of good manners so that he would

half rise by the time the visitor knocked at the door. An insurance salesman once dropped by, and my father rose and sank and talked to the man in a dreamlike state, and then discovered that he had sat on the man's straw hat and crushed it to pancake size.

I was more or less grown while my father worked Third Trick. I no longer kept him company down at the depot. I was off into the night myself. It was a time to carouse, to drink beer until it was cut off at eleven, then chase about in someone's car after girls or illegal booze or both, to swim in a cold lake with a gang in the buff by moonlight, to steal and ride a horse, to wind back home as a pearly light spread and get between the cool sheets a few minutes before my father's sober steps on the porch. It confused and frankly embarrassed me that my father worked nights at the depot when other fathers held day jobs and thought of themselves as important professional men. The depot seemed to have shrunk, too. There was nothing spectacular about freight trains whooshing through town at one in the morning. The men who wandered in and out of the depot were wizened and grimy and forlorn.

Yet I was irresistibly drawn to restep my father's path, to make amends to him for I knew not what by undergoing what he had gone through. The deeper part of me wanted to fight his enemies and his demons and to take his place in battle. I took a night watchman's job one summer at age twenty-one. He was now the one to carry my midnight food in a tin down to the building construction I was guarding on his way to Third Trick. I believe it was the same Christmas fruitcake tin I had carried to him as a child. He was chipper and smiling as he dropped it off and, I thought, proud of me. Other night people passed my way where I sat in a glorified wooden box on the edge of what was to become Kroger's Supermarket. A black man approached, booming loudly to me to let me know that he was there and not about to break the law in any way. He told me he would keep his eyes out for thieves, bummed a cigarette, and was off. A man with a cigar jammed in the side of his mouth burst in with no knock. I flinched. He had a slouch hat pulled down over his forehead and his eyes shone. All these night people had wide-awake eyes; mine, still day-oriented, were going out of focus. I took it that the man was in some form of law enforcement by his authoritative manner. He glanced about like a cop. He called himself a Security Enforcer; everyone else, I learned, called him the Door Shaker.

This man had private contracts with businesses in town to check through the night that no one had broken into their places. What he did was go through town and shake doors mightily. "I do it loud so a thief will know I'm there checking," he said in a surprising lisp. "Walk tough and they leave you alone." In a show of brotherhood he checked through the construction site I was guarding, although he was not under contract, throwing his strong flashlight beam around and shaking what doors there were. He came back to my plywood shack and told me his life's story. His wife had left him long ago, leaving him to bring up a small baby boy. He had raised this son on his own, coming in from night work, waking the boy, feeding him breakfast, and getting him off to school. It turned out that I had gone through school myself with this boy and never suspected he had no mother in residence, that he only had a father to turn to who worked nights. He had seemed no different from any other boy I knew from school. The Door Shaker told me abruptly that he had girl friends and just might send a spare one my way in the night. That woke me up, and for a stretch I anticipated a good-natured country girl being guided into my shack by the thoughtful Door Shaker. "Got to make my second round now," he lisped. "Keep your pecker cool."

During those long nights I worked as a watchman, the Door Shaker brought me coffee and doughnuts and spun yarns and gave me security enforcement tips. But he never brought along a girl. The one he had in mind was either sick or out of town. I read Willkie Collins in illustrated editions and daydreamed (nightdreamed?) about impossible plays I made on a mythical football team, the winning shots I sank in basketball, the girls who were astounded at my feats. I had no worries except to keep my eyes open and wonder occasionally about what a sudden creak from a pile of lumber meant. The construction bosses warned that they might visit me in the middle of the night, checking, but none ever did. I was left alone. I missed people and was always glad to hear doors shaking far off and know the Door Shaker would soon be with me.

I watched the sky gradually soften, show streaks of orange and then unfold in a blanket of blinding white. I tucked my Willkie Collins and food tin under my arm and walked up Boone Street Hill toward home. Newspaper delivery boys pedaled by, Mr. Winters on the Pet Milk truck stepped smartly to front steps with clinking bottles, and foot traffic passed in and out of the Appalachian Hospital at the top of the hill as if time of day or night had no real meaning. I saw a pool shark I knew as Blondie exit from the emergency room door in a white uniform of a hospital orderly. He was leaving the night shift, for he carried a lunch tin the same as I. He kept his eyes on the pavement and didn't greet me. He was one of Johnson City's leading pool shooters, gambling at nine-ball for as much as twenty-five dollars a game. In the poolroom, decked out in sharkskin britches, tasseled loafers, and a pearl-buttoned black shirt, he had a raffish, sinister air. It must have caused him agony to wear white and wade through the night emptying bed pans and wheeling stretchers. There were some people I wouldn't have been overjoyed to see either in my role as night watchman.

I walked in the front door, ate fried eggs, bacon and hot biscuits with a satisfied weariness and then made my way into the upper front bedroom. The sheets were at first cool in the early-morning breeze, but as I awoke from sudden bellows on the street and car honks, I found the bed heating up. The sleep process was reversed. At night it had grown cooler as the hours lengthened and the street noises had dwindled to nothing. Here, in the day, everything heated up and the clamor increased as the hours passed. I could only manage six hours tossing and turning, whereas normally I was an eight-hour man in bed, and I swung my feet to the floor with my mouth cottony, my back sweating and my spirit tired. I happily quit at the end of summer and went back to college. My father continued working nights until he was seventy, having put in fifty years railroading.

In retirement he reverted to sleeping nights without any difficulty, but he was a little lost in the day. He discovered TV and it helped somewhat, and he followed the baseball scores of the Giants. He lost interest in Dickens. When I was back visiting in Tennessee with a car, he would call on me to take him to see relatives and occasionally old railroaders. The sprawling railroad depot where trains used to whoosh by hourly was leveled like Carthage, its space concreted over, no trace left whatsoever. It only remained in the mind.

Once on a drive down a tree-lined street he told me to stop the car before a compact yellow frame house. I never had much interest in where he wanted me to stop; it was his trip. We climbed a long flight of steps and entered a cozy, much lived-in front room. It smelled of medicine. A woman who had the air of a nurse greeted us, followed by an old man with all his hair, and his figure slim and unbent. He had that happy, startled smile that many old people have when attention is paid them. "Come in, come in. Good to see you. Sit down, will you."

My father sat opposite the man, smoking a cigarette, leaning toward him. They talked of sports and physical ailments and railroading. "It's awfully good to see you," my father said.

"And it's good to see you, too. By the way, who are you?"

As we made our way back to the car, my father told me he had worked with the man for over thirty years.

My father eventually ended his days in the Appalachian Christian Village, a place given any number of appealing sobriquets—retirement complex, senior citizen villa, a place where one had the freedom of his own "apartment" but was taken care of in an emergency. It was a well-staffed, bustling place. It had a music room and a TV room and a large communal dining hall. No matter how you sliced it, though, it was a nursing home. No one had grown-up freedom; a nursery school and a nursing home have more than a few things in common. Visitors to this place moved as if witnessing a tableau removed from actual life, a Madame Tussaud's Waxworks of daily life. There were hearty, booming greetings—too booming and hearty—that wafted down the long halls and through the sitting and dining rooms, forced, strident bonhomie that one hears ricocheting around a nursery school. My father was not fooled. He knew—until his senses left him—that everyone was corralled in there to take leave of this planet. He saw the dark humor of it. He made jokes about the rapid turnovers in nearby rooms. (There was a wariness about making a new friend for fear one of you might not show up forever for the next get-together.) Someone would move in, be unloaded with great chipperness by loved ones who weren't staying, settle back among mementos, get in the swing of things, and die.

No alcohol was allowed on the premises, not even beer. Prayer was said before each meal. The food was uncommonly bland (said to be so because old people's taste buds were no longer acute), and no one ever seemed to wolf it down. I was introduced at mealtimes to the throng along with general-interest messages when I paid visits. My father got a kick out of my being introduced as "a visitor from New York." I looked around and saw men and women I had once feared and respected—now reduced to nodding before their soft vanilla pudding. There was the man who had sat in a banker's chair and once given me a car loan, over there a woman who had given me an undeserved B in arithmetic now staring woodenly behind huge glasses. My brother was traipsing down the infirmary ward hall and heard a free-associating line of obscenity. It had a rhythmic, distinctive pulse of its own, as grand as a drill sergeant's. He glanced in the room from whence it came and saw the mother of one of his old high school chums, a woman who had kept an immaculate house and fussed over decorum and well-balanced diets. She had been the most gracious hostess; now she might fling her feces at you, you who were still on the outside and free. "Send my son here," she said through the obscenities, my brother reported. "I am Mrs. So-and-So and I demand that my son be brought here this very minute. I want to know why I am being kept a prisoner. I am Mrs. So-and-So. Are you on the line?"

I was considering moving in with my father for a season, slipping in beer for us and reading Dickens, when the surgeon's blade descended and my father was not the same ever again. He went into the infirmary after the operation, and there was no chance of moving in and little chance of getting a beer to him. I was wearing denim clothing that season, and the Head Nurse—an amply proportioned woman in starched white and stiff manner—frowned on it, I suspect, along with certain alien points of view I might infest the place with. (In Tennessee denim was what poor folk, powerless folk, wore. Little did she know it was high chic in New York.) My father was talking rapidly then, fidgety as a teenager, and was the opposite of the patient, thoughtful man I had once known. I burst into the infirmary room the first time, ready to my core to do what was expected and what I had to do. The room had a curious scent of fresh sheets, Lysoled linoleum floor and a lingering aroma of an old man's waste. "Dad," I said, rushing in. "Oh, Dad. Don't forget we love you!"

"I don't want to hear anything about love," he said. "Before you say anything else, run out to the drugstore and get me a nose spray."

"A what?"

"A nose spray! One of those things you inhale! Go get it. Can't you understand it's important?"

He got his nose inhaler. I took charge—while I was in his room—of hoisting him to the toilet on command. He went a lot, but he didn't weigh that much by then and it wasn't too difficult to maneuver him. I showed up in early morning and stayed until well into the night, taking breaks when my brother or his wife took over. (They had been carrying the whole load before I got down from New York.) Some late afternoons turned out to be like old times. My father would tell an Ed Wynn joke and reminisce about how my mother liked to wear her hair long and straight down her back. He didn't eat, he didn't turn on the transistor radio except when I harangued him to do so, and he ceased caring about baseball and politics. Too bad—Watergate was just breaking, and he didn't get a chance to relish Nixon's grand troubles and fall from grace.

The Head Nurse wanted to move him to a psychiatric center —a loony bin. In our meeting, in her office, me in the denim of poor hill folk, she directed when I should rise and sit and talk. I told her, when my turn came, that my father was not going to a loony bin, that he was gravely, physically ill and at the end of the line. "He'll get better," she said. "He'd get better faster if he had proper psychiatric care. We're not equipped for that here."

I would, without a second's hesitation, have slipped in cold beer, but my father was taking pills of every color and shape and combined with alcohol might do God knew what. The doctor conferred with me by phone—when I called. He was a jovial, moon-faced fellow, someone I remembered well from the old days. He had been a few grades ahead of me in school and had worked hard to get into the hallowed medical school in Memphis. (Doctoring was the one sure, swift way to elitism in our hard-bitten neck of the woods.) He had driven a bus for a while in town before going to medical school (not so jovial in that role, as I remember.) Now patient after patient lined his waiting room, not a few elderly, health insurance and Medicaid forms much in evidence, having gray rubberized bands tightened and pumped up around frail muscleless arms and a cold silver stethoscope dabbed at white sunken chests. He was apparently making out well in the money department. He had bought a well-stocked cattle farm besides a commodious place in town.

He said, over the phone, that my father was responding well to medication. How did he know? Well, he checked with the nurses every day by phone. If something went wrong, he'd change the pills. It was like tuning a car—getting it to go just right. When was he coming out to see my father personally? Oh, well, he got out there to the Village about, he reckoned, once a month and saw all his patients in one fell swoop. (My father in the Christian Village, me in Greenwich Village.) Was there any likelihood that my father was going to die soon? No, not from all the reports he was getting. . . . I called him by his first name the way I had done in grade school and when he drove a bus. I wanted to believe him. I wanted to be reassured. I wanted to go back to New York for a week or two. "Yep, I'd say everything looks good for the next couple of months at least," the doctor said.

"Thanks a whole lot."

"You're more than welcome."

My father showed flashes of his old self. Usually it came just before we parted at night. "Now, son, you go on about your business. Don't you have things to do back in New York?" We told family stories to each other. The time I brought a Model T home, bought with paper-route money, and told him to "listen to her hum." The time my brother, as a little boy, climbed such tall trees no one could get him down. I wanted to ask him about real things—about him and my mother. About his struggles and jobs. Everything. But something held me back. Nights passed. Mornings I found my father seething, asking where I'd been. I'd hoist him to the toilet. He liked for me to do it rather than an attendant.

He began picking at imaginary threads. I'd never seen anyone do that before—plucking here and there at the bed covers. I said good-bye to him the last time in warm Tennessee sunlight. I shook his hand. He had been scrubbed clean; his bare feet showed no marks from wear or tear or years. They could have been a young man's feet. I looked at him and said, "Do you know who I am?"

"Sure I do. Of course I do."

"Who am I then?"

He didn't answer, but smiled and looked off in the distance. No one stayed with him that night—no family, no attendants or nurse. It was the way it had been at the depot. He was free. He took leave and died.

Three

Night light: the cool-white fluorescent of a fast-food shop, the incandescent bulb over a desk, the sodium vapor from a street-lamp. It is a candle's flame. It is the blue patina from a hiss of gas. It is the moon's pale glow. It is everything except sunlight. The hormone melatonin is released from the brain at night. Body temperature in sleep falls to its lowest at 3 A.M. Circadian rhythms tell us to sleep after dark and rise in early light. Yet people are often owls instead of larks, by nature and by choice. The Bureau of Labor Statistics say 10 million people work at night. Who knows how many of them are owls? Night is a strange country. It is mostly freedom from the day.

JOE IS THE NIGHT MAN in our apartment house. He wears an ancient blue serge uniform with white piping. He trots off in front of you to open doors and stab at the elevator button. He has a stiff-legged, slightly gimpy walk—like Shemp Howard, the bartender in *The Bank Dick*. He moves fast and nervously, unlike the day men, who can afford a confident amble. Joe is last man on the totem pole, lowest in seniority, relegated to the eleven-to-seven shift, beyond which lies the street and nothing. As he jerks the handle of the service elevator, sending it moaning down below, sighing first, he tells you once again the story: "I had no choice. They cut back on the doormen about eight, nine years ago, and I got bumped to this shift. I had days before. But you get used to it."

Face around to chuckle, eyes rheumy through heavily smudged specs. Little whiff of booze occasionally, stronger as the night wears on. "It was hardest at first just getting used to it. Now it ain't so bad. I got a schedule. I get home from here at

about eight, eat me a big breakfast and sleep for four hours.
Then I get up and do chores for the afternoon. Then I sleep four
more hours, have supper, and come here. You gonna be here
long in the laundry room? Just ring, I'll come right down. How
are the boys?"

"They're fi—"

"You just ring. Take care now." And he points a finger, like a
gun, and vanishes behind the hastily shut door. Joe vanishes,
invariably in a wreath of glad-handing, cigarette ash, and half
sentences. He is our weather reporter. As we lumber into the
foyer, weary in late evening, he will tell us what we have experi-
enced outside. "It's cold out there. Oh, brother. I hear the
temperature going down to fifteen tonight. Some lousy
weather. Next week we supposed to get some beautiful
weather. I hear. I hear that on the news. Now you take care.
How the boys?"

"They're fi—"

"They grow—"

Door closes. Joe's gone. Joe sits by the front door sometimes,
head lowered, hands between his legs, gray smoke twirling
upward from the cigarette between his heavily nicotined fingers. He could be crying, certainly he is sad, staring at the top of
his toes. I know depression, and he is depressed. He springs at
the nudge of your key in the lobby-door lock. His act begins.
"Beautiful night. Hear we're gonna have a streak of good
weather. Supposed to be up in the sixties. Can you believe it?
You take care now. How the—"

"Fine."

One night he stood outside, under the ripped blue awning
with white lettering, taking a smoke. He was giving himself a
taste of the weather—soft, fine breeze coming from the Hudson
River to the west. He sees our Volks station wagon pull up,
bicycles and boxes tied to the roof rack, back end a block of
suitcases, firewood, potted plants, hardware and toys. God
knows what's hidden in the front end under the hood. Both
boys' heads strain in the rear seats for release. One in a full-
fledged tantrum, already with his back arched, the other tug-
ging at his safety belt. Home from a country weekend. Joe sends
his cigarette to the pavement and grinds it out with his toe. It's a

doorman's nightmare. "Goddamn fuck!" Possibly he thinks we're deaf. Maybe it came out unbidden and irrepressible. But his act will not be stilled. "Good evening, Mr. and Mrs. Blowers. Beautiful weather we're having. How are the kids? There they are. *Here, let me have that!*"

Lowest on the pecking order, he will not risk a dissatisfied tenant in his playact. He must carry the first item out of the car. He tugs at a cooler in my hand. We wrestle on the street, and he wins. I'll let him win that one, but I'll have to be on my toes from here on. He is prone to dropping lamps and bags with cameras, slinging them into the service elevator, forgetting them in the hall, capable of anything while out of sight. At last, the goods wedged to the brim in the service elevator, kids writhing on the foyer floor, I say, "Joe, I'll get everything unloaded upstairs. Just watch the car for me, will you? Don't let a cop give me a ticket."

He is nowhere in sight, of course, when I return, car barren and mud-splattered and—thank you, God—miraculously unticketed. A night or two later I catch him. "Joe, what happened? I thought you were watching the car for me."

"Mr. Blowers, somebody rang. Somebody rang on a floor upstairs here. I gotta go when they ring."

He is caught between fears. He has his playact, but it can only run so long. There are rules, priorities and marginal duties to consider when day people intrude into his night. Management tells him that tenants must not operate the service elevator, period. Insurance laws, something. The day men couldn't care less. You could take the elevator to work with you. They are daytime sane. Night man Joe might have trouble lasting a full day shift now, for night dizzies the brain. He panics every time he catches you edging for the service elevator to operate it yourself. "Here. Let me take you down, Mr. Blowers," he says, listing sideways, as if on a rolling ship, coming on strong.

"No trouble, Joe. Just going down for a minute. I'll do it."

"Wait a minute. Hold on." He's got me. He's darted inside. We start down. "Beautiful weather."

"Ye—"

"Kids—"

"Fi—"

Now he's got to take me and two stuffed, hot laundry bags

back up on a grinding five-story ride. I do not know how old Joe is. He might be seventy or younger than I am. He is thin, a cougher, with unhealthy brown, parchmentlike skin. He gives himself good close shaves, his cheeks gleaming, his gray hair pomaded down flat on his skull. "Must be a Jewish holiday coming up," he says over his shoulder.

"How come?"

"Jewish holidays we always got good weather. Don't know why we always got us good weather then."

"You come from around here, Joe?"

"Born and bred. Lived my whole life within around five blocks a here. Yeah, I know the Village. Went to Technical High down on Morton. You know it? Jimmy Walker made us the speech when I graduated there. You know who Jimmy Walker was?"

"Ye—"

"He was a smart man. I remember it like yesterday. It was a wonderful spring day, you know. All of us were there in our best. Jimmy Walker told us some things I have never forgot." He turns, for emphasis. The elevator pings and scrapes as background. "I remember every word. Jimmy Walker kept a place on Leroy Street, you know, but he dint have to make a speech to some high school kids. He was a great man. They don't make Jimmy Walkers no more."

"What di—"

"He said," waving his hand as if conducting music, "go out there and be somebody. Now I know, everybody says stuff like that to kids. But this was Jimmy Walker. He had style—you should have seen his clothes. When he said it, it meant something. I never forgot that day. Here we are. Watch that door there. Here, let me help you. Let me have that . . . !"

Joe is Italian, part of an ethnic body being squeezed inexorably from swaths of the Village. They had first squatters' rights, like the Cherokee in Tennessee. Money came along—lawyers, youth, moxie and other people's strong desire to find enchantment there—to ease them out and on the road to Long Island. Peace treaties came along in the form of settlements for cheap rent-controlled apartments. Co-ops have sprung up. The iron ball hits the curlicues of tenements that still have the brass outlets for gaslights. An old Italian has been cutting hair for half a century—will give you a shave, a hot towel over the face and witch hazel as balm, somebody there to shine your shoes—and suddenly the term is not "barber," but "Hair Stylist." The new haircutters wear cowboy pants and Madras shirts three or four buttons open to the breeze. They carry their scissors in their back pockets. Music pulsates from bomber speakers. They charge twenty bucks a cut. One old Italian, I remember, tried to make the switch. He put a fly-specked picture of Tony Randall in the window. He stopped giving shaves, putting the cold razor to the back of the neck, and he let the witch hazel go. But he couldn't make the leap to jeans; a white smock never left him. He *scheduled* appointments. He kept a grimy white plastic radio hovering on an FM station where music of no particular bent or persuasion sputtered and faded, caught on for brief glorious moments, then died. Like the barber himself.

The old ones gather on benches in the concreted parks, warming themselves in the sun, huddling together. I've spied a nifty Joe there, on one of his afternoon breaks between snoozes. He's wide awake and calm and wears a feather in his pearl gray hat. He must have been born to be a lark.

Cats were born to be night creatures. They were born to romp through darkness, to skitter through the quiet when most of mankind sleeps. A good 60 percent of the animal kingdom is genetically attuned to live with minimum or no light. Better time for prey, better time to stay alive. To have to play with a ball of yarn or a rubber mouse in a sunny apartment while an owner pads around cooing affection is not in keeping with his natural circadian rhythm. Cats are happy in the tall grass at night, sniffing out food and foe. They are good-natured to put up with the demands of day, to turn their world around.

In animals sleep and staying awake are tied to survival. A lion sleeps through the day as does the gorilla, for who's going to attack? The giraffe takes only short daytime naps and can't risk closing his eyes at night. Everything is after his hide, and it takes him ten seconds just to rise. A blind Indus dolphin dozes in cloudy water for less than ninety seconds at a time, twenty-four hours a day, for it must keep moving to avoid catastrophe. The bottlenose dolphin puts the lights out in half his brain at one time, leaving the other half wide awake, and switching halves after an hour's time. The human need to sleep nights may have evolved from that atavistic period when to huddle together in a deep cave in the gathering dark provided the only safety against the large roaming cats outside.

In the Bronx Zoo there is the World of Darkness, where day is turned to night for the edification of daytime viewers. A man called Cosmo, a Senior Keeper, runs it. From ten at night until ten the next morning strong fluorescent lights burn over the cages—making it daytime for the bats and other nocturnals. They sleep. When the dim-colored forty-watt bulbs come on in the morning—nighttime—the animals wake up. Cosmo has become an animal lover in the twenty-five years he has been a zoo keeper. He loves the bats. There are four hundred of them in the zoo's World of Darkness. "Lots of people feel bats are creepy and are, you know, terrified of them. It's a myth. Bats are harmless. I walk into this cage every day where they are and they never bother me. Fact is, they're more frightened of people than the other way around. Bats aren't about to get caught in your hair or whatever it is that people worry over. They won't suck your blood out."

Night animals have larger eyes than day ones. Observe the owl. Their hearing is more acute. (Bats have an echo-locating system to help them find their way around.) No animal operates in complete darkness though—at least a sliver of dim light is necessary. And the circadian rhythm is so deeply implanted in all things alive that the sleep/awake cycle would continue along at approximately the same time in most of us even if we lived in total darkness. Our circadian rhythm. No one seems to know if it is in the genes, in the psyche or without rational basis. Look at an actual owl and you may be certain that he was born for the night. Look at a human being and you have no way of knowing if he's an owl or a lark. In 1729 an astronomer named Jean Jacques d'Ortous de Mairan conducted a novel experiment. He placed a heliotrope plant in a dark cellar. The plant went on opening its leaves in what would normally be daytime and closing them at night. It didn't need the sun or moon to tell it the time. The circadian rhythm persists in the absence of environmental time cues.

In the 1960s some deep-cellar experiments were done on humans. Scientists in Munich built a windowless apartment in the basement of a hospital. No timepieces, no radio or TV. No way to tell if it was high noon or deep midnight. The subjects had no contact with those conducting the experiment either, and they ate and slept whenever they wished. Around the same time a French scientist named Michel Siffre was conducting a similar study. He holed up literally in an underground cavern in the French Alps. Way within the mountain, with no natural light or communication with the outside, he soon had no idea of time of day or night. Both of these independent experiments showed that human circadian rhythm is a little longer than twenty-four hours—more on the order of *twenty-five* hours. Man—at least according to these tests—is not entirely attuned in his waking and sleeping to the position of sun and stars. He's on a twenty-five-hour schedule. Which means that left to himself, no alarm clock, a man will move one hour later into each new day. The result, in these two experiments, was that in three or four weeks a person lost one full day. Every subject was surprised to find that it was later than he thought—Friday, not Thursday; Monday, not Sunday.

The truth of this finding can be tested by anyone. During weekends, when most people are freed from the alarm clock, the majority stay up later and sleep later in the morning. The end result is that by Monday morning internal circadian systems have shifted an hour or two out of sync with solar time. When you get up Monday at seven and feel like death warmed over, your body may actually be at 5 A.M. You are not as refreshed as you think you should be after a weekend off.

It is impossible to fool the body though. The mind, yes; the body, no. In the Munich study some of the subjects tried sleeping longer than they did on the outside and tried staying up later. Some went on a thirty-three-hour day, sleeping thirteen hours and staying awake for twenty hours. Their body temperature, however, followed a twenty-five-hour schedule. Another important finding was that duration of sleep is most often determined by a person's temperature before tucking in. Subjects who went to bed as their body temperature was falling (as most of us do in real life) slept seven or eight hours. If their temperature was at its maximum, they slept for fourteen to sixteen hours. This happens indeed in the outside world. If someone stays up all night and all the next day until midafternoon, when his temperature is at its maximum, he will sleep a good sixteen hours or so barring outside disturbances. However, if he has been awake all night and then goes to sleep at 5 A.M. when his temperature is low he will sleep less than normal, only four or five hours.

Modern man takes gross liberties with the internal circadian clocks. Farmers go to bed with the sun and get up with the chickens—as it was done in the Middle Ages. Urban demands keep plants going around the clock, doctors on call through the night, police cruisers roaming through the wee hours. Nothing seems to work perfectly when the sleep/awake cycle must be changed radically. On U.S. atomic submarines which stay submerged for a couple of months at a time, the crews maintain an eighteen-hour day and night: six hours on duty, six hours asleep, and six hours off duty. Actual day and night mean nothing. Nearly all have problems with insomnia or broken sleep patterns and soon begin flying off the handle or developing some kind of emotional disturbance. Among enlisted men on U.S. atomic submarines there is a turnover of 33 to 50 percent—and only a handful volunteer for more than two or three of these ninety-day missions. Somehow officers on these submarines have worked out a twenty-four-hour schedule for themselves, and their turnover rate is much lower.

Most management schemes to get full use out of a day's twenty-four hours fall short of perfection. As we edge our way into the twenty-first century, more and more hours of the clock are being used. This presents a major problem to industrial, security and emergency services. The Stockholm police work shifts that start four hours earlier each day, and no one gets discriminated against or has his sleep cycle completely reversed. In Europe in general it is preferred to place workers on rapidly rotating schedules so they are on a shift for only a day or two at a time. No one's sleep cycle is fundamentally changed that way. There is discomfort but no major upheaval.

And then there are jets and eventually space travel where time takes on new meaning and the body is thrown into an immediately altered state. Internal circadian clocks can be shifted by an hour or two each day in either direction without much pain—but to turn everything upside down in a very short period brings on a newly coined malady to man, "jet lag." Adjustment is easier when flying west because of the earth's rotation around the sun. You arrive about the same time you left. You reach a place where circadian rhythms and the wall clock have been stopped while you've been in the air. To fly east is harder. You fly into the sun, to where the clocks are well ahead of your internal rhythm. You are exhausted, disoriented and stepping into no man's land.

I was briefly a jet-setter, and it was as disorienting as any experience I have ever had. It happened in the sixties. Clay Felker, a man in the magazine business, a rather unusual man, I've come to recognize, asked if I'd like to help put out a magazine in Geneva, Switzerland. It was an unusual period in the country, an unusual period for me, so I thought there was nothing very much out of the ordinary about it. There would be articles to collect, an office somewhere in Geneva, and a gallery of unknown people to meet. Nothing about it seemed odd. What was so odd about jetting to Europe in midweek, working a bit, jetting back to New York and working on a novel over the weekend? Wasn't everyone doing it? I was doing articles for Clay anyhow and the offhand, free-associating manner in which they were assigned and composed tended to condition me to the hallucinatory as the standard mean. He had sent me to Tuscaloosa, Alabama, to cover a football quarterback who'd just been signed by the Jets. I didn't know anything about expense accounts. I paid my own way. I'd only vaguely heard of the quarterback, Joe Namath. I cut corners by staying in Namath's apartment and tooling around with him in a convertible. I didn't exactly follow the guidelines of the Columbia School of Journalism. In fact, I didn't know any rules of journalism.

Clay merely breathed in the direction of an assignment as a way of commissioning a piece. "Ah, oh, there's a lot of mess in the traffic here in midtown. Why don't you, oh, ah, check out the problem. You can't drive a car through it or even park the car. Look around. Talk to the police." That was the assignment. It would become the cover story for *New York*, the Sunday supplement of the *Herald-Tribune.*

I had first come to Clay because a piece that *Esquire* had cavalierly given me had been just as cavalierly rejected (by Harold T. P. Hayes). I didn't ask or know about a kill fee. A friend I ran into on the street told me that *New York* might buy my piece. I called Felker. I'd heard he was married to a movie star and that made me nervous—the only thing about him that did. I got through to him in a second. He told me to bring my piece, which was about a young Tennessee boy who had recently landed a lead in a Broadway play, by the office. The office was a small partitioned space the size of an abbreviated living room. Steam pipes ran across the ceiling, hissing now and then. Typewriters from the newspaper side clattered away like distant gunfire. Clay was a man with clean-cut features, a distracted air, and a way of nervously running his fingertips through his sparse light hair. He read my piece in its entirety while I stood transfixed in front of him. His distraction left him when he read. He turned the last page, turned his head upward, and then faced me and said he would buy the article. I didn't ask for how much. It would appear the following Sunday. And in the meanwhile Tom Wolfe sauntered in in a nifty black outfit to sit and crack peanuts off to the side. So this was journalism?

I was cranking out stories left and right for him thereafter. And so another assignment, working on a magazine-to-be in Geneva, fell right into the hopper. "Go by and, ah, oh, see this ah, oh, man at the Hilton. He's pretty strange, but they tell me he's got a lot of money. We might as well see if we can't, ah, oh, get some."

I didn't care about money. I didn't much care about working. I went to the Hilton and met Bernard "Bernie" Cornfeld, because Clay Felker thought it might be a good idea. In a high hotel room that looked out over a hazy, blue-rimmed Manhattan, a smallish man with the torso of a peasant met me. He had a sensuous underlip and he smiled shyly and spoke in a soft, hushed voice that made him hard to hear. He also had a faint, vague stutter. He asked if I spoke French. I said I had studied it in Quebec for three months. He hired me. And I became a jet-setter—without a guide as to how one comported oneself when night was often turned topsy-turvy and there was no telling when one slept.

I only knew I was petrified of flying. (A few years before, on a theoretically easy flight between New York and Washington, the plane had dropped a few thousand feet in a few seconds, sending a few of us and our breakfasts to the ceiling. The stewardess broke her leg. I was never the same.) Since there were so many millionaires in the Investors Overseas Services-Cornfeld extravaganza, I ordered up a First Class ticket to Geneva. A member of the Cornfeld team, operating out of a back office with no name off Fifth Avenue said, "No, travel inconspicuously by Tourist Class. We all do—even Bernie."

He turned white and a small muscle near his eye began to twitch out of control when I told him some of my article ideas for the new magazine: "A Close Look at the Watchdog SEC"; "Where the Money Goes in Our Fund of Funds"; "Pen Portraits of Your Money Managers." He couldn't speak and I had to back out of his office. My first doubt about the legitimacy of the operation had arrived.

I drank many scotches before and during that first flight. (Felker couldn't make it this first trip. I was to travel to Geneva and start setting everything up on my own.) Our laden Swissair 707 rose lumberingly and everlastingly in early evening, straightened out, and flew head-on into a deep blackness. It lasted a moment, and then the sky beyond the gray aluminum wings turned a lighter gray. A few more scotches and a little rippling turbulence and we leisurely bounced into a snow-banked Geneva. I thought I saw John Kenneth Galbraith talking with I believe the dark-haired widow of a late President in the air terminal—as if in a dream—and then I checked into a Sigmund Romberg-type hotel. Still in a dream. My ears were buzzing, my eyes stung, and it was work making one foot follow the other. And one thought follow another. I had lost a night. It had been taken from me.

The next thing I knew, I was sitting at a board meeting in what looked like one of those preserved Vanderbilt mansions on display to tourists. There was mumbled talk, and then my acquaintance from the New York Hilton, Bernard Cornfeld, padded in and began talking softly about our proposed magazine. At first he talked in his usual soft manner. Soon his voice rose and the stutter left. He wanted a magazine that hyped his IOS mutual funds, that pushed products in its money market portfolio (whatever that was). The SEC be damned. We were incorporated in the Bahamas. We were doing big business in Europe. The pope bought stock, by God. We followed the law—no more, no less. My circadian rhythm, my internal clock, was grinding away at three or four yesterday morning. It was high noon the next day in Switzerland. I felt as if I were under water. My mouth was cottony. I wanted above all to put my head down on the burnished cherry wood table and shut my red-rimmed eyes.

I followed a board member to a café with a bright awning where, over *Beaujolais nouveau* and beefsteak, he diagrammed what IOS was all about. He did it in a sly, good-humored way. On a napkin he drew a narrow rectangle with its parts marked off in percentages to show where the money IOS brought in went. It was immediately clear to me, jet-lagged or no, that the whole operation was near criminal. We were in a W. C. Fields movie or riding down the Mississippi with Melville in *The Confidence Man*. When I was finally able to pry my lips apart, another person seemed to be speaking with my voice: "But, look here, someone comes to IOS to invest in mutual funds and most of his actual money goes right into the front end—into administration of the funds. Most goes to the man who sold him a share in IOS."

"I know," he said, with a devilish grin, happy to see I'd caught on so quickly. "So many people are dying to get into the stock market that they don't read the fine print. You sell it to them fast before they get a chance to think."

The new magazine was to go to these investors. I had been under the impression, from Clay, that we would make the magazine a tony operation. We didn't have to sell it. It went free to investors, it had a captive audience. Why not do good, readable stuff? It wasn't any harder to turn out. But how one sees matters over a quick coffee in a familiar threadbare environment in Manhattan is not the picture in a land of *Beaujolais nouveau* and board meetings in Vanderbilt-like mansions. I tried to give Cornfeld what he wanted. I barged into his inner sanctum of deep-piled rug, Regency furniture and a phone system that involved a loudspeaker. I buttonholed minions and clerks who turned out to be multimillionaires and tried to get usable copy about the benefits of IOS insurance or some mindless, unnecessary gadget in the IOS portfolio. In some degree of jet lag at all time, I often flagged in the afternoon and picked up at midnight. Cornfeld came to terms with jet lag—for he was flying all over the globe—by forgetting what hours meant. That was his answer. The office would be in a hectic state at one in the afternoon, ticker tape punching, men scurrying frantically with papers, secretaries dialing and typing like mad—and throughout, the words "Where's Bernie? We need Bernie to solve this!" And later still, at three perhaps, a puffy-eyed, freshly talcked Bernie would tread softly in with a petulant look. He didn't get fired up until dusk. Or he might change his mind, chuck it all, and fly to Paris—or Rome or New York. He once ordered Nathan's finest hot dogs flown direct from Coney Island to Geneva. Time or money ceased to mean anything to him.

He cherished and kept old friends near him—and newfound friends, too. He moved through the night spots of Geneva with a retinue. He didn't drink or smoke and had the constitution of a bull. He was especially fond of, and loyal to, members of his old Boy Scout troop from New York, of which he had once been the leader. One would come across a serene face in the operation, someone with clout but no work to do and ask who that was. "Oh, someone in Bernie's old troop."

Faces blurred along with time and the schedule one was on. To be involved in constant jet travel and lose the demarcated night is possibly more disorienting than deep-cave living. At least you know when you're in a deep cave. I thought I was in real life. I ordered lamb chops for breakfast on a craving and ate cornflakes at night. When I flew back, the sky stayed blue and when I landed I was in a semicoma for a while. I had no pep. I suddenly began laughing out loud for no good reason. And I wondered how the high and mighty of our government were able to fly hither and yon and keep—if they did—sane minds.

I could do no other work in New York. I could hardly get my laundry done. I saw a lot of Swissair, and I missed a lot of nights' sleep. One moment I was sitting in the Lamb's Club on a sunny, warm day with Clay Felker, discussing strategy on how to handle this hot potato, the next I'd be crunching over snow in Europe out to corner Cornfeld and his brethren. How did those Secretaries of State do it? How did they make those global decisions when jets knocked their equilibrium asunder?

Clay Felker flew in and out now as much as I did. Sometimes I'd be in Geneva and not know he was due and spot a figure in a tan military coat, snap brim hat, odd stare and briefcase. He'd be heading for a snowbank. "Clay, here—it's me!" We'd soon be setting up a dummy issue as we trudged in snow, as we had lunch or breakfast or whatever it was. We batted articles around on a plane, in a hotel room, on the street. As usual, I didn't know better. I thought this was how all magazines got started.

Bernard Cornfeld apparently didn't know any better about how to run a business. It all had a giddy, surreal ambience—like a party going on hours after it was supposed to be over. Nearly paralyzed with jet lag, I sat in Bernie's sumptuous office in deep cushions. They came, to and fro, financial managers just in from Djakarta, Hong Kong, the Virgin Islands. Anyone else might be there, too—a sunken-cheeked man with a movie script, a model in a bouquet of perfume or a mad racing driver. Felker might be there, doodling on a pad and working on a timetable and escape plan to Rome. A few times an important political figure from America entered the stratospheric air—a Roosevelt or an ex-lieutenant governor of Kentucky. Hubert Humphrey sent kind words—as if proposing himself for a seat on the board of directors when he stepped down from the vice-presidency. All sniffed carloads of gelt but none seemed to sniff the ripest of ripe scams. I got hysterical giggles at times. And when I found myself alone with Cornfeld, my jagged sleepless nerves were drawn tight. I had no idea what might happen. Suddenly, once, over the telephone loudspeaker, coming from nowhere, came the high-pitched squeak of Bernie's mom, who was ensconced somewhere in Geneva. "Bernie, I haven't heard from you in several days. Why haven't you been calling me? I'm a tiny little bit worried."

"I'm calling you soon, Mama!" he screamed at the machine. "Be patient. I know you're there!"

"All right, darling."

And once—as nothing seemed real in my sleep-deprived brain—Bernie lashed into me (and an absent Clay Felker). It came from nowhere. Spittle flew from the corners of his mouth. "No one *messes* with my clients!" We had offered a small bit of straightforward financial advice in our dummy issue. "You two New York jokers think you can put something over on me. You've got nothing to show me. Nothing!"

The following day, in his inner sanctum, he offered me a permanent job in Geneva for what sounded like a hundred thousand dollars a year. I was too shy to ask him to repeat it. I knew I would never accept no matter if it was a million. Escape plans went immediately into effect. I would abandon ship. How sweet then to walk by Geneva's lake in the sunshine, knowing I was leaving the final time. Severing all ties. I did a little jig, like the one Hitler performed for the newsreel after Paris fell. I in fact detoured through Paris before returning home, spending every last dollar and Swiss franc I had, cleaning out my pockets. I ate at Lipp's, because I knew no matter what I brokenly ordered, it would turn out to be beefsteak. I quaffed beer. To hell with wine. Free! Oh, God, free at last!

In New York I took long sleeps, got back on a day/night schedule and wrote a letter to Cornfeld declining his kind offer. I bowed out of his saga forever. It saddened me to hear later that he'd gone to jail for a stretch, his whole financial empire blown sky-high. I lost Felker, too, somewhere between Cornfeld's Fund of Funds and the founding of *New York* as a slick magazine on its own. I couldn't be a jet-setter or a follower of trends. But occasionally I miss those times in the clouds.

Left to my own devices these days, I take the subway—finding myself with a start occasionally in a far, lonely stop in Brooklyn in the wee hours with an interminable wait and no earthly soul in sight. But I like the rattle of the subway, the sway, the plunge in and out of tunnels. I like the yellowish sandy light one sees outside the windows. I even like to catch a whiff of a special smell it has which is evocative of a bygone New York.

Now and then I do take a taxi. And tonight in one I run across an owl. He is driving it, and I sit up front beside him while the three people I'm with take the back.

"Where'd you get that hat?" he asks.

"It's an Irish tweed," I say, taking it off and showing him. I feel duty-bound to talk to cabdrivers, having briefly been one myself. "You can crumple it up like a cap. Wash it. You like it, eh?"

"I like to know about stuff like that," he says. He is a moon-faced black guy, sunk 'down on his spine, in gold-rimmed glasses. He drives uncommonly slow up Sixth Avenue, hand limply guiding the wheel. We are caught in a blaring glut of traffic at Herald Square. The weaving taillights ahead are dizzying.

"Must be easier driving a cab in the day."

"Wouldn't know," he says, beginning his tale that lasts from Macy's to Lincoln Center. "I never go out in the day if I ever can help it."

He grew up in the North, but he had relatives in the South whom he stayed with during summers. (It is not an unusual ritual for a lot of black people marooned in the North with southern ties.) "My grandmama kept our family together. We just congregated from all over on her every summer. Now here's how I got hooked on being a what-you-call-it night person. I grew up being a kid like everyone else—you know, rising early in the morning and going to bed a little after dark. My grandmama was strict on the children. She made us hop in bed. I was about nine, I guess. But the older boys down there, a lot of my cousins, got to stay up. . . .

"I remember being in a dark bedroom and knowing they were out there having fun. I could pull the shade back and see the country store down the road. That's where they sold white lightning, you know, and pop and things. Lights was glowing there. People were laughing. I never forget those lights, how all-fire alive it was. And there I was having to stay in bed. It done something to me. I had to have them lights. And when I got old enough so my grandmama couldn't keep me in bed, I began living in the night. I tell you the truth, I hardly gone to sleep any at night since then. I'm up throughout it."

My driver says he drives the cab through the night, five times a week. On his off nights he stays up with television and a few drinks straight through until first light. "The night has a lot of moods on the street," he tells me. "It has its quiet times—like right before sunup. And it has its troublesome time—when the bars let out around three and people are drunk and weaving all over the place. It's like Fourth of July then. I know this city perfect at night. I know street people."

"Anything bad happen to you?"

He tells me two stories. He picked up two boys one night and they robbed him at gunpoint. As they walked off, he took his own gun and shot each in the back of the head. "I really hated to do that. I can't forget it and I mourn it. But one thing you got to make your mind up to driving a cab here at night, and that's that you're willing to die if somebody's about to take your money. That way you can live with driving a cab—just say, 'That's it, I die or *they* die.' It simplifies everything and relieves you of a lot of tension. 'I die or they die.' Nobody takes my money easy. I got my gun stashed right here."

Another time he was suckered out of position by a pretty young woman. She wanted him to take her from midtown to Harlem right after the bars closed. Normally he wouldn't honor such a request. "But I felt sorry for the young lady, you know. She said white cabbies wouldn't take her and she had to get home. She seemed fine and dandy. And I thought I'd be a Good Samaritan and help her out. I like to help people. I get up to the address she named, and a guy stuck his head in my window with a gun and got my money. I'd been set up, you see. I didn't shoot that guy in return, but after he got my money, I ran over him in the cab. I was waiting to get him in my sights and when I did, I gunned the motor to the floor. He was lying there in the street with his head next to the wheel. I just damn near run over his head, but I stopped. Know why? I wouldn't have got my money back then. Everything would have been too messy for me to get in his pockets and get it back. That's what I thought. So as he lay there knocked out, I get in his pockets and get my money back. The girl run off. Those are some of the things that happen at night."

"Does your wife mind your being away at night?"

"My wife understands how I am. She may like it or not like it, but she's got to understand. That's me. Something else about me. I like women. I see one standing over there and she appeals to me, I might go lie with her. That's the way I am. I never throw it in my wife's face, but I like me some strange every now and then. That'll be four-fifty. Thanks very much, sir. Now you all have yourself a fine time tonight!"

We have dinner at the Ginger Man. The impresario of this evening is, as always, our good friend Seymour, the restaurant reviewer. As tasters and "cover," Lis and I go along on these gastric nighttime adventures. We do not pay. We could never pay. We have been to Lutèce, Alfredo's, Le Périgord, Le Veau d'Or, La Caravelle, the heart of Chinatown, the depths of Times Square. We enter as hearty, bona fide, deserving, well-heeled trenchermen. Good evening, Mr. Maître d', I'll have a martini! I wear (everywhere, any season) my springtime Paul Stuart suit, Brooks striped shirt and a pair of Brazilian loafers with a dime-sized hole on the bottom of one of them that no one will see unless I forget and cross my legs. All of these warmly lit, lightly buzzing spots meld. There are vases with freshly cut flowers, strategic mirrors, clean starched linen and heavy, important silverware. Those who serve bend to our whim. It's a far cry from the all-night diner, the haven for owls. Those at other tables flash gold cuff links and confident smiles. No one bolts for the door; there is no braying or strident tongue. Everyone seems to have just taken a bath, especially the help. The food is endless and there is always the richest and lightest wine to wash it down. No one smokes. They were first to get the word that smoking will kill you, not to mention that it ruins the *sauce béarnaise.* They go on to nightcaps in homes well above the roar of traffic—or at least one supposes.

We go back to the Village. Joe has just come to work. "Good evening, Mr. and Mrs. Blowers. Good evening, Mr. Britches, Miss Conkton. Windy weather!" Tobacco floats around him, his eyes bloodshot, a faintly sour smell emanating.

What separates you, Joe, I wonder, from those who flash gold cuff links and tear into frogs' legs Provençale? What turn did they take—*you* take—that made you open doors and push elevator buttons at night and them crawl between clean, freshly ironed percale sheets in the cool, safe dark? Your world and theirs—night and day.

Four

THERE IS A RACKET from the service elevator past the walls. Joe collecting garbage. The refrigerator comes on, the oboe to the elevator's bassoon. I'm awake—though still half in the dream about being back in the State Department, knuckling under to my old burr-head boss. This dream recurs: night after night I'm forced to do what I don't want to do. I snuggle into a ball and take a quarter of the horse blanket. Our door opens and there is a hushed, complete silence. A gentle breeze comes in its wake. Somebody stands in the doorway, somebody whose head just about reaches the height of our bed. Spiderman in tight, blue-striped pajamas. "Mommy, may I please come to bedwidyou?" We have taught him manners. He says please. Lis hugs him. She usually takes him back to his bunk bed by hand. She will pour him water on command and even croon him a melody. "No, David," she explains oh so softly, sleep-ridden. "It is the middle of the night. You have your own bed. This is our bed. Please go to your own bed." A wail, like a sudden wartime siren erupts, that of one sentenced to the torture rack for life, not a mere bunk bed. *"No! No! No!"*

"He's waking me up! Keep him quiet down there!" from the top bunk. Two wails now, in syncopation.

At last, fifteen minutes later, only low, intermittent groans come from the bottom bunk bed. . . . Let's see. An advance could come after the second rewrite on "Men in Bed." Oh, men in fucking bed! The granite block of bills due stands majestically in the dark, illuminated in my mind like the 20th Century-Fox logo before one of its movies—klieg lights flashing around it. A very small safety net lies under it, something the size of a dish-rag. . . . I've batted back a host of assignments from the place, wrought pieces that might even have wearied Norman Mailer and brought him to the mat. I've done chocolate, the cocktail hour, women of the Wild West, women bankers, hillbilly girls, clairvoyants . . . and female jockeys yet, for Christ's sake. I did one on jockeys! I've written them all, served in their trenches like a shell-shocked vet. . . . And I weakened and took what they call a relationship piece—"Men in Bed." I let it be plucked out of their fat assignment book—a tome of little précis that reads like Arthur Bremer's diary.

I knew, oh, I knew that a woman who hangs upside down from a bar on arising at dawn would never like what I said and knew about men in bed. The piece would finally break me. . . . She turned down the first submission—not even insertions would work. Goddamnsonofabitch. Maybe they're mad about the two grand sent by mistake. Their mistake, now their displeasure. For comfort's sake, let's haul out billets-doux of the past, her legendary notes to contributors. ("You are my most favorite writer. You string out prose like a Cartier necklace. Your fan, Helen.") Wheww! Who is she? She takes the bus home after work—not a limousine, not even a taxi. The bus. She drops to the carpeted floor in her office and sends a secretary out for Dramamine. Bill comes to a dollar nineteen. She reaches up for the bottle and says, "Did you get a receipt?" For tax relief. . . . Oh, poor woman. Will you ever know ultimate relief?

What turn does one take in life to depend at this crucial moment on a magazine with the same nonface on the cover each month, the same articles inside? The same faces running the operation, too, month after month in their cubicles. Faucet goes drip-drip-drip. Got to turn it off or it'll drive me crazy. Take a leak while I'm at it, aiming at the rim so lower bunk won't be alerted. Think of the literature courses, all the books read, the minds revealed. Think of those novels typed in barren cells. The places I've been, the people I've known. What turn did I take, what turn? The first assignment came so easily so long ago—a frivolous moment in time, but the first shot of dope. Now I live to depend on it. . . . I need that money to pay the bills!

What do men do in bed? Break it down in categories. . . . There are macho lovers, passive lovers, kinky—oh, how about the roll-'em-over-quickly lovers, the ones looking at their watches? The interminable lovers. . . . The interminable sluggers, the interminable buggers—oh, Lord, it's getting away from me. . . . What about the artist lovers?

Duke Ellington was an artist. He worked after everyone else went to sleep. On his art. The rest of the time he was into scat and the con. He slept in hotel rooms and he never slept at night. "I'm a night person," he told me once. "There are just a few of us left."

Summer of 1967. Duke sits backstage at the Carter Barron Amphitheatre in Washington. He has his stockinged feet propped up on a stool, belt and pants undone to allow a big belly room, and around his head a do-rag to keep his greased, touched-up hair conked. He has the most enormous pouches under his eyes I have ever seen, bulging cushions, a cartoon tribute to sleepless nights. He tilts his head back to administer eye drops every so often, to fuel the bags.

Everyone pays him court, a whole line of people. You do this by bending and kissing him twice on each cheek. I do it and get the feel of sandpaper from the bristle of his beard. "My, my, aren't we looking sweet tonight," he says, grinning and pleased, to a plump woman in a tight pink dress and flowered hat.

"Duke, I knew your father right here in Washington. I went to school with your son Mercer right there. I remember you coming through Washington on your way to Paris once. You remember me?"

"How could I ever forget? Let me tell you something. There ought to be a law that says a woman can't get as beautiful as you."

"Go on!"

The door closes behind her and Duke says to his graying son, Mercer, "Who the hell was that anyhow?" He makes Mercer spell the name and then shakes his head. Men all around him for the moment, he tells about an experience he once had in a Paris brothel. Two women doing an *exhibition*. Sometimes these women cheat. Not on the Duke. He peered deeply and made sure he saw tongue on labia. "There was going to be touching or no payday. Hey, hey, they got paid!"

"Five minutes, Duke!"

On stage he comes out striding, in a ruffled purple shirt with heart-shaped cuff links, in a tuxedo. The crowd in the large open-air theater goes wild with each bit of business. He puts the microphone by his mouth, looking soulfully out, the huge bags beneath his eyes glistening in the spotlight. "Listen. We love you madddddly!" The orchestra plays the ones they want to hear—"Satin Doll," "Mood Indigo," "Take the A Train." There is no telling how many times he has done these standards. He could do them in his sleep, if he ever slept.

We are in his suite at the Hilton, the hotel where Reagan was later shot. The large retinue dwindles and the hour grows later. Young female singers try out for him. He is the soul of encouragement. A TV crew flings itself here and there, lights glaring, making a documentary on the Duke. I get into a fight with the man doing the documentary, his horning in on my interview. Our words grow hot. Duke loves it. I stay the course, and it's finally the Countess, a seasoned blonde with a pleasing European accent, the Duke and me. The Countess is his Constant Companion. She has a little white poodle called Do Do.

The Duke loves junk food—all junk food. He abominates air conditioning. Won't have it. Dreads flying. He feels at home with Room Service. He has a Coke and puts sugar in it. Other times he has a cup of hot water and sugar with a dab of lemon. He likes steak, but tonight he makes do with two cheeseburgers, followed by a bucket of ice cream. But first he prays. Prays over the cheeseburgers, gives thanks, and asks God's mercy. Out of earshot the Countess tells me, "The reason he's becoming so religious is that he's scared of dying."

The Duke wears a red silk bathrobe that comes down near his ankles and a do-rag. He consults with his New York doctor, Dr. Logan of Harlem (later a suicide), every few hours by phone— listing his minute-by-minute state of health. He says, "That bell captain made those cheeseburgers himself. You know that? He didn't go out for them like he said and use the money I gave him. He did it himself in the kitchen on the sly, and he pockets the sum. I know every ruse there is. I've worked every club."

The Duke has a portable electric piano. After everyone drops off and he is finally alone—usually around four in the morning, but sometimes when it's even light again—he composes. Every day of the year. He writes symphonies, operas, suites, dirges, church music, beautiful scores which fill box after box. It is his art. The familiar routines, the I-love-you-madlys—are a scam. I ask him why he just doesn't go to sleep. He's done enough.

The Duke hardly ever answers a question directly. The reply comes back elliptically. "I'm looking for heaven, always have been. We're all looking for perpetuity. And heaven is a lot of blazing lights way off there. . . ." He is telling me this at around four-thirty in the morning. He moves his hands a lot and chuckles like a down-home Southern preacher. "We want to get to those blazing lights. But all the way to them are holes you can sink through. They get you and you fall . . . to the *other* place. There are so many cutoffs around those lights. I'm trying to get to those lights."

He is talking about Art. I put aside, mentally and physically, my notes. My mind goes elsewhere. A whole kaleidoscope whirls deep within, not at all soothing. The feeling is that I have an appointment to be elsewhere. Maybe if I were holed up in a furnished room banging out a novel, I would feel differently. But here I am in a hotel room, the dim clatter of china sounding from Room Service, a shuffle of feet and some yawns. Balzac said adieu to the world at midnight, pulled the velvet drapes and stayed up all night with strong black coffee and his furiously moving pen. Marcel Proust finally retired to his cork-lined bedroom on Boulevard Haussmann in 1907 and wrote through the night. He hardly ever stirred outside. He had, let's not forget, a private income. John O'Hara stayed at the Pickwick Arms when he first came to New York. He roamed the streets and hit the saloons in the early hours, and then when things began winding down in the gin mills, he retired to one of those boxlike rooms in the hotel and wrote away on *Appointment in Samarra* through the night—hardly making a correction in his copy. He didn't rewrite. Came dawn, he crawled under the blankets and slept till late afternoon, to begin the process all over again. He wrote about where he had come from in Pennsylvania. It was Art.

Little did I know when I wolfed down *Appointment in Samarra* in the sticks that I would come to Manhattan and check into the Pickwick Arms by chance first thing. I didn't know O'Hara had made the same choice. All I knew was that it was miraculously located in midtown on the East Side, a perfect spot, and that its rent was just about as cheap as the Y. It also had rather diminutive rooms. In mine my feet went out the open window as I lay in bed. It had an arrangement where two rooms shared a bathroom in the middle. It involved a lot of locking and unlocking doors. I would lie in bed, feet out the window on a warm night, and listen to the other party brushing his teeth, gargling, and giving the toilet a quick flush. What if it were a woman—a young actress come to try her luck or a model or a finishing school grad. All I hoped was that it wasn't a fellow Tennesseean. I wanted to leave the South, kit and caboodle. I wanted dimly—the way Duke Ellington wanted fundamentally —to be an artist. I walked the streets of New York and probably kept up with O'Hara in the number of frequented bars. But when I returned to my room, groggy with the sights and smells of the grand city and full of Nedick's hot dogs and beer, I drew my knees up in bed and looked at the shadowy water tower on a far rooftop. I did not try to write about where I came from. I slept.

Not all accounts of night wanderers are accurate. Does Jerzy Kosinski tool around town, peeking in on the after-hours demimonde? He is reputed to be out till dawn observing the raw nerve of the city? I have no idea. Who can find him? You can find Andy Warhol—or used to be able to. He was said to roam through the night. He was one of my earliest magazine assignments. I found him in his place of business—the Factory, it was called—off Union Square in early evening. A stuffed Dalmatian was by the door, Cecil B. De Mille's former dog, and a gracious man in a dress took my trench coat and introduced me to the silver-haired artist. Warhol had unhealthy-looking skin, and he held a tape recorder up for me to speak into. I didn't mind. It was impossible to ask him a question and get an answer anyhow. He moved like a pale ghost through a speckled and plumed array of young and recently young people—all rhapsodic about where they came from and what they were up to. Warhol merely observed and used. He went home around midnight to his mother, with whom he lived on the Upper East Side. He practiced Catholicism.

The ones then in his orbit threw themselves with great verve through the night—as if it were always high school graduation night. The evil there was composed of ignorance and innocence —and was not Mephistophelian. The sweet man in the dress, the most feminine of any in the gang, took me aside and told me his story. He was Jackie Curtis, and he was the offspring of a New York taxi dancer and a sailor passing through New York. His grandmother ran a saloon on the Lower East Side. It was all a little strange in the nether night world of Warhol's band, but superficially I was on familiar ground. I was talking to an agreeable, flirtatious young woman. She (as he and Holly Woodlawn, a Puerto Rican lad, liked to be designated) wanted to make sure I was comfortable and did I need perhaps a little wine? I accepted a paper cup of weak rosé. "I like to take my shoes off and get comfy at the end of the day," Jackie said.

She had large feet. The hair under her arms hadn't been shaved very well, as revealed in her sleeveless, sequined dress. There were several runs in her hose, and a pungent locker-room scent wafted from her. Her makeup had caked in spots and her mascara ran. She batted her eyes and her hands flew. I asked where her father came from and did she keep in touch. "He comes from Elizabethton, Tennessee. Real hill country, darling. They'd never seen anything like me. But I did the best I could when I went down on a visit a year ago, and my father did the same. It must have been a trial for him."

I thought in a panic that she might have oracular powers and knew that Elizabethton was my old neck of the woods. I used to bicycle over there on hot summer days. It had moonshine and fundamental Baptists and a history from frontier days when Davy Crockett wore coonskin. Now on a New York night a man in a dress was telling me his father came from there. I didn't tell her what I knew of Elizabethton. How could I be a hip reporter of New York nightlife and know about such a remote, tiny Tennessee town? Hell, I was taking notes and sporting a turtleneck. And I moved off to see what else was in the world of Warhol. A very short young woman with a mass of hair falling around her eyes cornered me. She'd heard I was there on a story. "I am a

Star, Mr. *Cosmo*. You're required to write me up. Put me on the cover!"

This was Andrea April Feldman. She had on a leather jacket, jeans and boots. She craned her neck back to look up at me, sweeping a mane of blond-streaked hair back. She didn't laugh at anything she said, no smile to hint at any humor behind the stagy, outlandish spiel. Only Warhol smiled—and occasionally Paul Morrissey, his colleague in cinema. Andrea began phoning me at two and four in the morning. There was no preamble, no introduction. She didn't even take time to say who she was. "Mr. *Cosmopolitan* Man, I want to know if you're going to put me on the cover. I'm the only star in Andy Pamby's operation. The others hover. I star. Listen to what I tell you. I went to Streisand's concert and stopped the show. Who else in Warhol's menagerie would do that? No one else has the guts. I did a showtime right in the middle of one of her numbers. It brought down the house."

"What's a showtime?"

"You'll see."

Sometimes the phone would ring and there would be silence on the other end. I would wait a moment, then say, "Is that you, Andrea?"

Pause. "I'm the greatest."

We met one evening when she was to show me the nighttime rambles of the Warhol crowd. We met in a crowded Daly's Dandelion on Third Avenue. I heard her coming up through a mass of heads and shoulders before I saw her. "Hey, Mr. *Cosmo* Man." She carried her passport to prove she was old enough to drink. I saw by it that she had been born in April—hence, her middle name. A parent had had a quixotic moment at her birth. She talked through a drink and a stagily smoked cigarette and through a cab ride down to Max's Kansas City on lower Park— taking time out to kiss me in a frenzy in the cab, stretching her back out stiff and straight and shutting her eyes hard. She opened her eyes in mid-stride. "I'm going to do a showtime tonight. You'll see!"

Max's was where the Warhol crowd hung out. That season it was physically hard to get into the place. It was like the Coupole of Paris in its heyday—jammed with energy and youth and extravagance and a minuscule portion of art. Today it is boarded up and dark inside and the wind swirls debris by its door. This night Holly Woodlawn and Jackie Curtis meandered around in dresses, Joe Dallesandro showed off his muscles and tattoos, Jane Forth stood icily with her plucked eyebrows and rouged cheeks—everyone greeting one another, bussing cheeks, crying "darling," just like at Sardi's. Warhol wouldn't stay up late—he was dispatched soon to his home. Nearly everyone else was good for the closing hour of four or dawn. Many had been in *Trash*. They had become part of Warhol's coterie, had walked into the Factory and got themselves into a moving picture. They got immediate attention; it had been amazingly simple. They hadn't been paid anything, but they had got their names in lights—for a moment.

"It's SHOWTIME!" Around two in the morning, in Max's Kansas City, Andrea suddenly leapt onto a table in a wide-brimmed hat. She began taking off her clothes. First went pants. Then a fishnet blouse. She shook her breasts. "It's shooowww-TIME!" Management—or some force—was bearing down on her. The table groaned. She fell backward and glass shattered. Hands pushed her back onto the table. She only had her hat on. "Show—" And she went over, not to return to the tabletop again.

"If she tries that once more, she's had it here. I've warned her the last time."

She reappeared shortly—clothed—and acted subdued and weary as a prize fighter might after a grueling bout. She had been performing. Showtime was not easy. It was her contribution to art in her time. And now it was growing late. A year later I heard she had jumped from the top of an apartment building in the Village. She left a note which said, "I am heading for the Big Time."

In Washington I take out my pen and pad and listen to Ellington once more. He tells me he is sometimes mistaken for Cab Calloway. He likes to be. He doesn't tell me, but I know he has an honorary doctorate from Yale. He has conducted symphony orchestras at La Scala and in Hamburg and the NBC Symphony of Toscanini. He wrote the score for *Anatomy of a Murder* for the movies, *A Drum is a Woman* for TV. He has met every President in his lifetime except John F. Kennedy. In a White House receiving line he kissed Nixon on both cheeks and told Pat Nixon that "no first lady should be prettier than a certain degree, and you are exceeding the legal limit."

We stand before the window that looks out on Washington and the late-night sky. The Duke grew up in Washington and loved his mother dearly. The night he learned she had died, he burned the clothes he was wearing. "I know the night but not the day," he tells me. Others have told me he never sightsees when traveling. All his life is lived at night. "You've heard of the rainbow people see in the day?" he asks. "Well, there's a moonbow you can see at night. Look out there hard enough and you can see it. See?" It still looks like just the moon to me. Later, near dawn, he speaks of another phenomenon: "There's something I call the Cellophane Sky. It lasts for only a couple of seconds and it comes just at the crack of dawn. The sky has a quality that's just like cellophane." We watch as the sky lightens with first light and ever so slowly turns from a gritty gray into flashes of gold. "You see it? It was there. You see it?" It looks like just another dawn to me. I am bone-weary and dry-mouthed. Duke is fresh and happy and going off to compose on his electric piano for a short while before turning in.

The Duke is dead. *The Saturday Evening Post* that commissioned me to write about him has passed away, too. I used to fly to Europe and Hollywood on *Post* stories. I bought a cabin in the Catskills with a couple of *Post* paychecks. *Cosmopolitan* never used the stuff I gathered on Warhol. It printed my stories on mushrooms and women jockeys and a chocolate factory. . . . The door swings open. Silence, as the breeze rushes through and rustles the curtains. "Please, Mama, may I come to bedwidyou now?" It is still dark, but the digital clock relentlessly jumps forward in time. Five o'clock is the magical moment when David may enter between us. Four forty-one. Close enough. "Bottle. May I have a bottle, please?" I creak out for it, stiff-leggedly, in the manner I remember my father reduced to in his last days, and return. I stare at the ceiling and wonder how much truth I can work into "Men in Bed." It helps one's self-respect to work in just a touch of the truth—a paragraph, a thought even. A warm spot spreads beside David. His Nuk nipple on the intake, leaking fluid. I reach down and feel a wet circle coming my way. Day breaks.

Five

A strange thing happens about once a week in the windows of New York's grand shops—at Saks, Bloomie's, and Bergdorf Goodman. It happens at night. Elves in the form of graduates of the Fashion Institute come in and change the displays, putting the finishing touches on as the light outside turns steel gray and trees can be distinguished in Central Park. It happens as if in a dream, as if a silent, magical hand had passed over the windows, day people unaware it's unfolding. Pink mannequins thrust bony pelvises and long swan necks at new angles and don creations forever kooky and excruciatingly stylish in yet one more novel and unique environment—all doomed for revision in seven days. These artists, whose work never hangs in galleries, learn to live with the brevity of their creations.

NEIGHBORHOODS CHANGE CHARACTER SWIFTLY as night descends in New York. As I roam streets familiar by day, I feel I'm stepping into a no-man's-land. Bed at three may bring on the sweats, but the pavement at this hour in Manhattan brings on shivers that go up the spine, cause quick head swivelings and a fast stride. As Dr. Johnson said about the situation of the man about to be hanged—it improves the power of concentration as nothing else does. Forty-second Street at midnight has few stragglers this night. The iron grills are rolled down over the novelty and gizmo shops. The porno emporiums are shut. Theaters featuring such fare as *Rear Admirals* and *Nympho Cheerleaders* seem to be dealing with at best one or two customers. Management in the form of black men in cheap mod clothing loom at doors and look bored and at the same time furtive—no mean feat. I hear steps. A man in Hell's Angels garb, keys

jangling, a wiry black, is overtaking me on my right. I cling to
the curb. He is talking crazy: "Hey, bob-a-re-bob. My dolly lives
over the ocean. Hey, man," to theater doorman, grinning, "you
showing spreads in there? Any pinks?"

He continues his greetings like a burgomaster up the street.
Any merchant open gets a howdy-do. He circles around and
comes back my way, a boomerang. He is too happy, snapping
his fingers and doing a little shuffle every so often. Coming
straight on. At the last moment I give room, a quick sidestep. He
may or may not notice. "The Communists goin' come, man, and
clean house here. They goin' shake some ass. Look out!"

Eighth Avenue bubbles on through the night with hookers
and drifters and crazies lurking and marching along. The un-
mistakable tourist can't help looking up at the tall buildings and
being a little stunned. His clothes are too neat and his expression too open for the terrain at hand. On Broadway, the Great
White Way, the same roving foot traffic seems duplicated, the
lame and displaced and exotic rubbing shoulders. It is as if an
agreement had been made that Forty-second Street itself
should now be considered off limits, perhaps too publicized, too
worked over and mined. Give it a wide berth.

Enclosed in a steamy restaurant on Broadway, the help move
in a slow trance. A waiter with dyed hair and a ramrod-straight
back regales coworkers with anecdotes. He is white, they are
black. "I take my little Tallulah out for pee pee every morning
when I get home"—eyes roll among the audience, hee-haws
booming—"and you never know what's going to happen. I'm
holding her in my arms yesterday when this e-norrr-mus fat
lady comes up. She's got rings on up to her elbow"—hee-haw,
hee-haw—"and she looks up at me and she says, 'I don't know
which of you is more beautiful. I don't, dearie.' " Hee-haw, hee-
haw. "I say to her, 'Listen, doll. Why can't you be a hundred-
seventy-five-pound stud. Then I might believe you.' " Knee
slaps and rippling hee-haws. Down the counter comes, "Mo
coffee here." It comes from inside an overcoat. A head is somewhere in there, too, bent over the counter. The confab up front
dries up, piqued put-upon expressions everywhere, and a
counterman in a smudged jacket peels himself away to pour
coffee for the overcoat, his hand shaking and spilling some in

the saucer. It's as if the rituals of night do not include efficient juggernaut service. This place bustles by day.

On the street a strikingly pretty young woman, taffy-haired, in sensible modest clothes, looks ever so slightly my way. She seems to be lost on her way to Scarsdale. She has the look of an undergraduate at an expensive, stuffy girls' school. I come near. "Hello, handsome. Want a date?"

Things must really be getting tough all over.

"I work the midnight-to-eight shift, and I love it," says Ormond in the Milford Plaza on Forty-fifth Street. "If you want to get ahead in the hotel business, the fastest way is to work nights. I wouldn't work any other shift."

He looks at me intently in his office with no windows—where it could be high noon or three in the morning. He wears a blue suit and a white tie with blue flowers sewn on. He smokes continually. His eyes are bloodshot in his dark-skinned face. He comes from Barbados, where he began in the hotel business at twenty years of age as a waiter. He left a son and daughter and wife there to come to the United States. Now he lives alone, in Brooklyn.

Working nights means you become a manager quicker. Not that much competition for the job. At night the Muzak that pulsates through the lobby is of a faster tempo than that of the day. It perks people up, gets them moving a little quicker. You need it as a stimulant. The problems are different at night— more drunks, tempers a trifle shorter. Businessmen try to duck in at three with popsies in spiked heels and lacquered hair. Ormond must intercept and delicately bar the way. He seeks to keep the hotel quietly running through the night, like a ship in murky, somewhat dangerous waters, to hold the lid on the raucous and touchy. A guest now barges in to shout that his luggage hasn't been brought down from his room. He's been waiting thirty minutes. Told it'd be down in fifteen. He wants an answer, a vein at his temple pulsing. Ormond fixes the problem in a second, gliding away and back, saying, "People lose conception of time at night. They think it's been an hour when it's only ten minutes. That was nothing to solve."

Thieves have tried to steal the lobby rugs—had them rolled

up and halfway out the door before Ormond nabbed them. He has caught them carrying a five-hundred-pound statue away. A man checked in and stayed drunk for a week, night and day losing meaning and demarcation. He came in at four with two young, pretty men. Ormond intercepted. "It was for the man's protection. We don't care about private lives. But I sensed trouble. I told the man so." The man said that he wasn't staying in a place where he couldn't entertain his very best friends, where they weren't respected. He was going elsewhere with his friends. He wanted a drink. He came back in the morning without his pants and not knowing where he had been.

Fires break out at night in hotels. It is the time for suicides. Ormond remembers wistfully a honeymoon bride who fell from a high story at the Taft. Hotel people are intrigued by suicide, are specialists in its trappings. "I keep my eye out for a potential one," Ormond says. "They come in without luggage. That's one sure sign. That and that they want a high floor where there is nothing between them and the ground."

Ormond goes smiling through the night, solving problems here and there, keeping on top. He has no trouble staying awake but has some going to sleep when the time comes. He rides the subway home to Brooklyn and is there by nine o'clock in the morning. He first has a big meal, which he still calls "breakfast," and then he unwinds. He roller-skates, jogs and plays Ping-Pong. He does errands and takes care of personal business, and finally sometime in the afternoon when there is nothing else, he goes to sleep. He awakes at nine at night and has another huge meal. He has only two meals a day, and he is back at work a half hour before his shift starts at midnight. He once went three months without a night off. He does not take a meal during the night, hardly takes a break, always primed for a problem and incident. He is getting ahead. The only days that really bother him are the big holidays like Christmas when he wishes he had family to go home to.

Distant clinks and a vacuum cleaner sound through the night in the hotel. It is an enclosed world with no one hurrying. You have your job, you do it at your own pace, no one looking over your shoulder. Ormond glides from floor to floor, across the lobby, in complete equanimity. Theresa stands by the computer in an alcove down from the front desk, smoking. She is the night auditor and she is twenty-four. She wears the loose white sweater of a homebody, red slacks, and she peers through heavy, large glasses. She shifts ledgers around carefully, seems a little guarded, and you realize immediately that here is a night person. Day work would turn her frantic.

"I can't work days," she says solemnly. "I've known I wasn't cut out for the days since I was about eleven. My mother worked nights at the Commodore in payroll and I kept her company then. I found I liked people who were up nights better than day ones. I'd rather be with night cleaners than in an office during the day."

Theresa is divorced, has a young child and lives with her mother. She works from eleven to seven, five nights a week. She is home in time to feed her child breakfast and get her to school, is up to welcome her back and stay with her until bedtime. She leaves after the child is asleep. "I see her more than if I were working days."

Theresa has rituals through the night. She has tea at a certain hour. The bartenders and restaurant help bring their receipts in on the nose—looking weary, ready to go home, nothing like the quick and busy souls they'd recently been at work. They are obvious larks. She jokes with them. Fox-trotting Muzak bounces off the wall; the computer terminal hums. It's as if we're all waiting for something to happen. "I once saw an actual suicide," Theresa tells me. "It was just after daybreak. I came in this room where some back-of-the-house people were congregating. 'Back-of-the-house' is what we call the clean-up people. Anyhow, I show up and someone immediately says, 'There's a body out there in the courtyard. Go look. He just jumped.' They were always kiddin' me, telling me things like that. I say, 'Oh, sure.' And I look a little closer and see a man as if all the bones had been taken out of him. Blood all around. The ambulance was on its way. . . ."

Outside the hotel the stoplights glow down Seventh Avenue —a long streak of green that is gradually turning into red far down the horizon. It is a marvelous ride on a motorcyle at this late hour—no traffic, the feel of the power in being able to open the throttle full, like being on the runway at Kennedy International, a green border on both sides. I used to do it down Fifth, on a Honda 175 CC, from Harlem to Washington Square, trying as if in a game to see if I could never be stopped by red. I played by the rules, though, and stopped when a red caught me. The driver who once did screech and slide behind me was not playing by the same rules, actually was not obeying the law: "Goddamn, son. Let me tell you," in a heavy Spanish accent, breathing in my face after jumping from his heavy sedan. "You must nebba stop on red like that. Somebody close behind gonna piledrive you from rear. Oh, son, you like to die then! Don't drive motorcycle. You get killed stopping on red like that in New York City."

I flag a taxi tonight, and it is the compleat late-night cab driver. You never encounter this type of driver by day. Only a slow, late hour, wiggling neon and a certain zany exhausted feeling in the air brings him out. He would evaporate in the sun —or be collared. "Hiya." We streak down Seventh, windows open wide. Beside him blasts music from a formidable black machine, so high in decibel that its tune is lost and one doesn't know if a vocalist is there somewhere or not. The driver is on something, and it is not something with a quiet, soothing effect. His head flies from side to side, long hair swinging like a mop— to the music? to some internal sound? Stoplights mean nothing. We part the traffic before us, a wall of sparkling taillights, as if we're a missile. It's an unlikely missile, a Checker that rattles from top to bottom. We stop a yard or two from the curb, motor racing, car still rattling. He turns and presents a damaged, late-night face, teeth broken and discolored. He smiles, and he wears a dirty olive-drab Windbreaker, an army issue. I pay. He is off in a wild lurch, an oncoming car swerving aside. This is not an unusual ride or driver at a late hour in Manhattan.

How different the night is in New York compared with the South. I remember the long, curvy roads of east Tennessee, the late nights there. They were lathered with fog, the air brisk and sweet as I drove in complete assurance of time and place. Going home for a hot bacon sandwich, a glass of cold milk and reading *The Naked and the Dead* till dawn. Firm-skinned girls would always be around to date—the system of dating would continue forever. Marriage was for elderly people.

But it was transient, as that carnival was in Lynchburg, Virginia. And artifice seems more natural at night than day. It's better to be drunk then—and carouse. I ambled into a girlie show at the carnival in my trench coat, some folded, lined yellow sheets in my pocket along with a Flair pen. On assignment. I caught the early show, the first of the evening. It was an all-black ensemble. This was the sixties, when a cheerful debate flared in New York over the use of nudity on stage. The no-name, ragbag, roving carnival was staked out in the place where the Moral Majority would later make its headquarters. The tent had a musty, highly used scent mixed with fresh grass beneath that evoked Boy Scout trips and circuses. The sides of this tent showed patches of wear and tear. I witnessed a line of rather ordinary-looking men—with a couple of exceptions— enter. They matter-of-factly pressed against the apron of the stage, a few good-naturedly nodding at others, most with faint smiles. A frenetic black man in a do-rag came forth presently on stage and made a snappy roll on a snare drum. "All right, here dey come! Give 'em a hand!"

Four young ladies raced out from nowhere in brief spangled costumes, turned their rears and wiggled them for the audience. The men increased their smiles and politely clapped. The women flew off out of sight in a welter of giggles. The MC strode to the edge of the stage in mock anger and raised a drumstick high. "That all you want? You don't want no more?"

The paying customers had apparently been through this routine before. I had myself long ago. We were to pay an additional fifty cents and then see the real goods. It's called "dinging them" in carny lingo. I chipped in happily. Another more prolonged drumroll, and the women tore back in a shriek of giggles —all naked. They ranged in color from coffee to ebony. Their pubic hair glistened under the lights, and the lights were not turned down. I thought the performance near completion. But no. The women passed down the line of men they were slightly above, and the men went to work. All were indistinguishable from those one might spot any hour on the town's main drag— save one, a man in leather apparel and a broad-brimmed gaucho's hat, someone who brought to mind Christopher Street near the Hudson. Apparently the men had full rights to do what they wanted with what was in front of their eyes. Lo and behold, one citizen stroked the morass. With no preliminaries and no apologies, another worked some digits in. The gentleman in the gaucho's sombrero went all out. He smothered one with his face, his hat dropping back on its chin strap. Up and down the line they were taking turns. And still being polite. A particularly stocky black chorine put her hands behind her head, jutted herself into an apple-cheeked man's face, rolled her eyes and said, "Eat that thing, man!"

The Saturday Evening Post had sent me down here. An American institution. It had been delivered to my home in Tennessee, where I had wolfed down Pete Martin articles that began, "I call on so and so." Their editorials went out to the heartland, exhorting the grass roots to do good. Well, here I was in the heartland. Assignment: Take a look at a small, roving carnival and report back. I moved right up close to get a better look. To my horror the MC in a do-rag shot before me and raised the drumstick over my head. "You can lick it, brother, but you can't fuck it!"

Then he trotted back to his drum set and ran off a roll. The men had their fill and afterward filed quietly and politely out of the tent. I saw other girlie shows. I saw one in which a slender blonde with near translucent skin performed; her husband was a dour and narrow-eyed man, the barker and MC. They were the total team. He made a solemn announcement in the tent before the performance began. "Now Miss Kitty will do her guaranteed full show, walking right along there for each and every one of you boys. But, let me tell you, if she gets pulled down off the stage, this show stops right then and there."

The man looked us all over. I met his eyes gravely, letting him know that I was there in a serious quasi-sociological role, above it all in a way, not there to muff-dive his wife. I had met him an hour or so before at the carny motel. His eyes had been roving the terrain even back then. Now Miss Kitty in nothing but high heels took dainty steps along the apron of the stage to the tune of "A Pretty Girl is like a Melody," and members of the audience did so well what they had done in the other tent. I saw this one, and I went to see Smokey perform. Smokey was really Jean, the mistress of the owner of the carnival. Many boys were in the audience here, mouths agape and eyes glowing in wonder and happiness as an actual woman lay back before them on stage and proceeded to smoke a lit cigarette between her legs. She went about her business in an effortless, professional way, swatting some of the more eager and curious boys away as if they were flies.

I talked to Preacher, the owner, about these girlie shows, telling him that some of the stuff boggled my mind. How was he getting away with it in the Bible Belt? Didn't the city fathers complain? "They want it to be hotter," he said, unsmiling, a look of burden on his shoulders. "They tell me, 'More, more.' Couldn't I let the girls go a little further? Only time I got a complaint was when this mayor in a little town in Georgia came up and said, 'I know I told you to make it hot, but you got to tone her down. My district attorney is down there eating it every night. It don't look right!' "

We were on the battered Ferris wheel and I had put my notes away. The rattletrap creaked us up and then whooshed us down. It was made to turn by what looked like an old truck's motor. At the crest I looked out over a dark, pastoral scene past the lit midway. The air was heavenly. It was calm and quiet and sleepy past the carnival gate. But my mood of contemplation was soon broken by the discovery that the wheel had gone out of control and was revolving at breakneck speed. "Stop us, stop us," Preacher screamed to the boy in charge, a none-too-bright, towheaded youngster. He was wielding a crowbar on the truck motor, and we were flying around now with air beating against our faces. No other passengers were aboard, proving the prescience of the locals. "Stop us! For God's sake, get us off!" Metal began to scrape, and an eternity later our feet hovered a foot or two above the earth, the contraption stilled.

My notepaper kept coming out less and less until it and my Flair pen were finally stilled also. My hours and consciousness turned topsy-turvy. I lay in bed in the carny motel and heard Jean and Preacher come in the room next door. The walls were thin. Jean's voice was strident and tough and ever complaining. "There Lester was doing it right out the trailer door tonight,

pissing up a storm. Like to hit a couple of people. You got to fire
him!"

"Right out the door?"

"It ain't funny! And that nice boy from *The Saturday Evening
Post* here and looking."

Silence. Then: "Smell it." Pause. "Go on!" Then mad giggling.
And soon: "Take it!" And, "Ahhh!" I tried to picture what was
happening, and couldn't quite. Glass shattered and furniture
moved. . . . And up and down the walkway in front of the
motel, carnies moved through the whole livelong night. Who
could sleep or want to? Lester the Fixer held court in a far
room, an uncertainty prevailing as to whether he had rented it
or taken it over from someone. He was sought after and sum-
moned others, bawling out carnies who had let him down, praising others, trading drinks and swapping yarns. He lay back on a
bed like King Louis XIV—only in his drawers, not ermine. He
particularly lashed out at a shambling youth with bad skin and
broken, dirty nails. "You let me down, Leon. Goddamn, you let
me down. I can't understand it. Here I give you two hundred
bucks to drive the truck and I haven't seen you for two weeks. I
was counting on you."

"I can't understand it either, Lester. You've been good to me.
Try as I might I can't figure it out. I just took off with a woman
and spent that money. You don't deserve to have that happen to
you. Could I have a drink?"

"Here."

I expressed interest to Lester about a young carny girl I'd
seen working the midway earlier. Did he know her? She had
raven hair and alabaster skin and a sweet, shy look. She had
been running a gambling game. My fantasy was to bring her
back to New York, send her through secretarial training and
introduce her to the finer things. Play Pygmalion. "That's
Cherry," Lester said. "She's part of the Mackey family. The
Mackeys are all carnies, right up to the great-granddad. Her
granddad remembers when carnivals were lit by torches.
There's nothing she won't do. No drink she won't take or pill
she won't swallow. She's done everything. Don't be took by that
innocent look. She'd turn you every way but loose. She'd fuck
you till kingdom come."

I felt my reason ebbing and a strange attraction calling. Just party through the night. Join this happy band and throw off all social and legal restrictions. Say you're one of them—be "with it"—and you'd never be tied down. You'd never pay taxes or own a credit card or need one. I plunged right in, even doing a turn as a shrill at a gambling store. But I never made it to the farthest rim. I never made it past being an Honorary Carny. I never became a card carrier.

And suddenly one morning in Lynchburg it disappeared. The tents came down, the trucks moved in and the carnival without a name moved on. I went back to New York and tried to write it up for the magazine. It didn't work. But what did it matter? The magazine sank and disappeared itself. I like to think of the carnival still roving out there in the sweet countryside, the bright unshaded lights still twinkling against the dark.

I understand that Eric here in New York, an editor for a girlie magazine, himself a sedate, bookish and kindly man, had a heart-stopping encounter a few apartment houses up from mine the other night late. So safe-seeming our middle-class neighborhood, no excitement other than our landlords trying to gouge us in a hundred-thousand-dollar co-op deal for our meager two bedrooms on a charming, tree-lined Greenwich Village street, near all public transportation. Safe. Right around the corner from Balducci's and the Jefferson Market and landmark churches on Fifth. Eric was coming in by cab from a late evening out and decided at the last moment to grab next morning's *Times* around the corner. (The joy of the big city, to be able to get next day's print the night before!) Eric had walked this street thousands of times before. So safe. There was the black grillwork, the wisteria vines over brick, the easy, snug steps to town houses, the warm glow from inside, the glimpse of books rising from floor to ceiling, tasteful, expensive art on the walls.

" 'Scuse me, mister, got a match?" The two men were quite well dressed, had stepped smartly from one of the brownstone stoops. Eric hadn't given it a second thought. It was such an ordinary sight. Then: "Give me all yo money." Eric saw a nickel-plated .38 in a dark hand. He stuffed a hundred dollars from his front pocket into someone's free hand. And they were gone—no trace. The police told Eric he was lucky to have been carrying the hundred. He satisfied them quickly. Anyone with a gun can shoot you quickly if dissatisfied.

Death can tiptoe in so easily. An extra set of tennis and a coronary grips you. A sudden quick decision to grab the *Times* late at night, to walk this street instead of that. A knife comes out, a gun is raised. Night is the time to fear spooks and think of death. There is "Hansel and Gretel," which I read to Nick—children going into the foreboding dark forest, Hansel dropping white pebbles in the moonlight by which to find their way back home. I used to run home in Tennessee, up the middle of the street, after the poolroom closed at midnight. It was no New York, but I ran hell-for-leather down the asphalt, eluding robbers and demons and shadows. It seemed sensible. At nights in the country now, at 3 A.M. of a cold winter's night, I wake hearing the odd creak by a far window, the sudden scurry of tiny feet across the roof (a squirrel?), the lonesome howl of the wind. Raccoons scratch at the screen. I have nightmares up there of Death in the form of a bear, standing on hind paws by my bed, waiting to pounce.

Of course, sleep is our foretaste of death. In bed, asleep at night, we are all more or less equal—as we will be in the grave. No one reserves a special Concorde flight in sleep or a table at Lutèce.

Six

I AM UP FRONT in a police squad car in Manhattan. Behind the wheel sits Sergeant Artie Cappabianca, a stocky man with a bandit's mustache. He chooses nights to work because he's paid a higher salary than for day and that will help him buy a house. Policemen and firemen—men thrown in the jaws of death constantly—have a conservative side when it comes to financial matters. They risk their hide daily the way no Wall Street high roller ever would, but they wouldn't dream of risking their retirement benefits, and they need the security of steady pay. They seek the perks—the night differential, the early retirement, the sick benefits, no less than any civil servant. They will not take risks with paychecks and bonuses.

Cappabianca wears a bulletproof vest, which his wife gave him for Valentine's Day, and carries a .38 strapped to his ankle plus the one at his waist. A shotgun, ready to go, lies snapped in a metal brace on the floorboard of his squad car. Another reason Cappabianca likes nights is that it's the best time for what he calls "hunting." In the day you get a lot of petty stuff—someone asking directions to Rockefeller Center or a three-card monte game to break up. At night the real desperadoes come out.

We cruise down side streets looking for car boosters, for they like to go to work in the small hours of the morning. We spot two men on a long street that has industrial plants on either side and no homes, the perfect stretch to break in a car and loot. No one should be coming around here to catch them. A line of cars, lit fuzzily by the overhead streetlamps, are parked against the curb. One man, in a white, armless undershirt, carries a satchel. They have spotted us; one yawns and stretches, an attitude of nonchalance. They stroll in no hurry to the corner, turn and vanish. No trace. "You have to catch them in the act or with the goods," the sergeant says, "or they're gone." He guns the squad car around the block and comes back to the same corner. It is quiet and eerie. Suddenly a loud, sharp rap sounds on the squad car roof. A wild man is poking his head in the window. He has come from nowhere. "Hey, Officer, how about a ride down to Avenue A and Third Street?"

"Who are you?"

"Me?" He pokes a finger at his chest. He is drunk. "I'm a neighborhood boy."

"Get lost. What the hell you think this is? A Yellow Cab, for Christ sakes?"

The drunk raps the squad car, harder this time, as we move off. He wiggles his hips and sticks out his tongue. The sergeant's face flushes, but he must forebear. He is not out at night in a squad car with a shotgun to hunt drunks. Every fifteen minutes or so he calls a squad car under his command over to check out paperwork and find out what's going on in his territory. He does this by drawing alongside the other car, sticking up his well-worn operations book, and making a scratching movement against it. He wants to see, as they call it, their "scratch." One blond, affable officer ambles over to the squad car, and the sergeant reaches in back and pulls out a toy space gun. He fires it, the gun going off in a crackle of flashing blue and yellow and making a beep-beep. My son has one like it. The blond officer puts his hand to his chest, rolls his eyes, and pretends to sink. Then he straightens and cheerily hands over his "scratch." This is a regular routine they go through—kidding the material, so to speak. They gossip some and give each other their impression of how the evening is going. It seems to promise a very quiet night.

The sergeant drives back and forth, up and down, within the boundaries of the 13th Precinct, which covers Manhattan from Fourteenth to Thirtieth Street, Seventh Avenue to the East River. The back of my calves are cooled by the shotgun's muzzle from below on the floor. A woman's voice, with Southern black overtones, keeps coming over the squawk box in a rasp with reports of in-process crimes and trouble. On a rooftop at Bleecker and Tenth Street—in the 6th Precinct—a man has been spotted with a gun. On the southwest corner of Washington Square a man is stopping people with a knife and making indecent gestures. He is identifying himself as a police officer.

We are winding our way up Third Avenue, caught in a wave of shifting red. Businesses have their heavy gates pulled down over windows, but a few bars and coffee shops are lit and bustling. During the day the sidewalks here are mobbed. A slightly menacing calmness spreads out now, into the shadows and behind shut doors. Sergeant Cappabianca swivels his head, his glance going up a side street, lingering over a man standing idle on a corner and loafing. There is a roar of traffic to a red light, then that deceptive calm while a wad of traffic waits for the signal to change.

The sergeant has a way of suddenly cutting down a side street, speeding for a hundred yards, then crawling to the next corner. He changes his speed, he tells me, to disconcert any would-be perpetrators of crime. They won't know if he's coming or going. The sergeant is one alive man now, his glance never very long anywhere. He doesn't yawn. He's looking around while he talks softly. He has all the characteristics of the big game hunter in the woods, who listens for the snapped twig, the object that moves slightly when it shouldn't. Only once has the sergeant hunted for animal game; he fell through the ice and never went back. "Look there," he says, jerking his head. "That guy crossing the street. That's one of New York's finest burglars. He must have just got out of the slammer. I got to tell the guys."

The white man is in Bermuda shorts, a knit cap pulled to his ears, and he wears a huge pair of sunglasses at well past midnight. He carries a quart of milk in a paper bag, perhaps something he needs for morning breakfast. The sergeant tells me that the man's entire family is involved in crime—mother, father, brothers and sisters, grandparents. We drink him in, and cut again down a side street that is adorned with low, mean-looking hotels. "Want to see something interesting?" he says. "Watch."

A string of women in skintight skirts and slacks and jump suits, leaning against buildings, pausing in doorways, standing on corners, begins to disappear. It is as if an invisible hand wiped them away into nothing. As we approach, the street is crowded and chattering—the next moment, in a split second, nothing. Prostitution is currently the bane of the 13th. It started during the Democratic National Convention of 1980 when prostitutes along Forty-second Street and near Madison Square Garden got the word that their presence would not be appreciated while the politicians were in town. They moved downtown to the heart of the 13th and have been there ever since. They work through the night, as Sergeant Cappabianca does. "You see these guys who pick them up and you wonder what's going on," the sergeant says. "They look like average, decent men. Businessmen with briefcases. Where they come from I'll never know. They just show up at three in the morning and get one of the girls. You'd think there was enough free stuff around as it was."

We drive on, slicing through the night. Sometimes, the sergeant admits, it gets lonely being out in the squad car alone. It's not bad having company tonight. Now is a pleasant moment. The squawk box has stopped rasping, and a soft breeze comes from the East River. The sergeant can't totally keep from hunting and he slowly winds around a parking lot, on the *qui vive* for any brothers who might be cooping. He stops on a small strip of concrete overhanging the river which looks like the set for *Dead End*. Foghorns sound; the air is still. "Get out. Take a look," he tells me. "This is one of the best views in Manhattan." The Queensborough Bridge stretches across the river before us, and there is a tall blanket of light from buildings along the curve of the Manhattan shore. Manhattan looks a lot different from the way it did down the side streets we'd just been cruising. Here you see its immensity, get some idea of the multitudes who crowd its island space. You get a sense of ants at work, building stupendous edifices and countless wonders that they themselves may not be aware of. "You know, this would make a great photograph," the sergeant says, taking off his hat. When he's not really working, he takes off his hat. "When I have a minute and I'm nearby at night, I often come here just to look. I bet you could get the right photograph and sell it. I don't know anything about photography."

We climb back into the squad car and move out slowly. Most

of Manhattan seems asleep, most apartment windows dark. Little traffic now. I scoot down lazily on the small of my back, but the sergeant's eyes keep darting. Suddenly the voice of the squawk box says, "Ten thirty-one," and is lost in a rasp and sputter. The sergeant hears more. He grabs the hand mike and puts it against his lips. "Where?"

"Gramercy Park. East side. Hispanic with machete. Inside the apartment."

The squad car takes off, floorboarded, tires squealing. My head is thrown back. The adrenaline surges. An apartment—someone in there with a machete, taking off heads, crazed enough to come at us, too, from behind a door. A motorist runs a red light in front of us, but the sergeant can't stop to give a ticket. "Son of a bitch, I'd like to have got him," he says. The sergeant takes corners on a dime, guns it down the middle of deserted blocks. A block from Gramercy Park he cuts his lights. The hunter does not want to alert anyone he's there on the scene. He wheels in quietly, stopping several houses from where the wild man may be swinging the machete. It is too quiet, almost no sound now. He takes his shotgun, flings on his hat and trots toward a row house that faces the green park. It has wrought-iron grillwork in front. A late-night dog walker and a lone stroller stop and gaze as the sergeant passes them with his shotgun pointing at the sky. . . .

I had met the sergeant about four hours before. He had a firm handshake but surprisingly small, delicate hands. He wore a strong, sweet after-shave lotion, and he stood before me a bear of a man. Part of his girth, I learned, came from the bulletproof vest he had around his chest. Cops can be mistrustful at first, but once you pass muster they can be charming and solicitous, funny and irreverent. You do not want to be on the wrong side of them, though; their natures can change. The sergeant instructed me in the proper squad car behavior before we took off on our night run. "Roll up the window on your side and lock the door anytime you leave the car," he said. "And don't ever get between the shotgun and someone if we're outside on the street. Promise?"

"I promise."

Before taking the squad car out, he ran his hand lightly over the back seat, down in the crevices, over the floor. "Got to make sure no one has shoved a shiv or anything back here. I've found everything back here. We take a prisoner, we don't want him pulling anything on us."

When we pulled away from the warmly lit station house at midnight, it was like leaving the cozy hearth. We were soon alone in the world, cruising side streets. And the sergeant told me about himself. His wife was a nurse and they had no children. His wife was not overly delighted with his having night duty, but she put up with it. They had long, leisurely dinners before the sergeant took off for his shift. The sergeant liked to cook, stuffed fish a specialty. He was an amateur railroader, holding a brakeman's license. On days off he traveled to some out-of-the-way line with a steam engine and took runs for the fun of it. He built bookcases. He looked forward to vacations.

"My father was a civil servant just like me," he said. "He worked for the post office, and he taught me that a man has got to have job security. But I never, never in a million years, thought I'd end up being a cop. I guess I thought I was too liberal or something. I just applied for it because it seemed to offer the best career opportunity at the time. But I've never forgot the way my father used to get up at the crack of dawn every morning for work. I never wanted to do that. Day people, you know, shut off the alarm and race through breakfast and off to work. Working nights you get up at your own pace, have a lot of time to do things before leaving home. One of the really satisfying things about my job now is seeing other people going to work just as I'm getting off."

He told me that he once wrote a book about police work with another policeman. It took them three years. "Boy, what greenhorns we were," he said. "We didn't know anything about agents or editors or publishers. We wrote it. It was the truth, things that had never been put on paper before. Innocent lambs that we were, we just sent it out, to this publisher and that, to TV shows and movie companies, to anybody we thought might help us and give us a break. Know what—know fucking what? They stole all our fucking book. They picked it clean. They got away with grand larceny. For a year we kept seeing our scene and situations and whatnot turn up on TV police shows. Our stuff was so special that it wouldn't have been a coincidence! We got taken. I felt like the biggest dope in the world. Here I know every scam on the street, every device a crook can use to rob a victim. I know the Murphy game inside out. And here I was being taken as if I had hayseed coming out my ears. . . ."

The sergeant practically squirmed in delight when he explained how much he liked to hunt thieves. He had made over three hundred personal arrests—"collars," they call them—some hairy; he broke his hand in a fistfight once during one. He had eight citations—a lot—one of which was for hauling the residents out of a burning whorehouse. He had labored as a patrolman in many precincts of the city. He had been on the narcotics squad. Never once had he been seriously hurt. Each morning he expected to get through the night and take the twenty-minute drive home to Bayside, Queens. He drove against the flow of traffic, as most night workers did. He liked to have a snack in his empty apartment when he got there, and wind down. He told me he slept about five hours each day. . . .

Now he carries a shotgun and comes to the stoop of the house on Gramercy Park. There is no shell in the chamber and the safety is on—but it would take him but a fraction of a second to load and fire. A blast would take off a human head at three feet and down someone at a hundred yards. Two women stand at the top of the stoop, one in tears. "He took her gold rings," the one not in tears says. "He knew immediately where the gold was, I don't know how."

The man of the house is at the top of the steps, looking nervously up and down the street, hands on hips, and is keeping up a brave front. He wears a casual, long-sleeved sports shirt and has soft, genial features. He would seem out of place where violence is concerned. "He was just suddenly there," he says. "We look up, and he's there. I go after him, and he grabs a machete on the hall table and raises it over his head."

"Who's machete was it?" the sergeant says.

"Mine."

"Did he take it with him?"

"He did."

We get a tour of the large first-floor apartment where lights are on in all rooms. Cartons and stuffed green plastic bags are piled in hallways and there is a scarcity of furniture. We learn that the people are in the process of moving to Florida. Sergeant Cappabianca discovers that the thief got in through a rear bedroom window that had been left open a crack. He looks behind every door, his shotgun raised and primed. At the end of the tour other policemen enter in no hurry and the sergeant turns the paperwork over to them. We stand in the foyer by the beveled glass of the front door where the man of the house points above him to a large, jagged hole in the ceiling. "Somebody got in a month ago and ripped the chandelier out," he says. "This fellow tonight, we just looked at each other. He was in my house, suddenly there. I didn't know what I was doing. He grabbed the machete and held it over my head. I got him by the seat of the pants and flung him out the front door. He went down the steps. That's the last I saw him."

"Will he come back?" one of the women wants to know.

"No, he won't come back."

The man begins telling the story once again as we leave. On the street the sergeant says, "Shit."

"What's the matter?"

"The guy got away. I can't stand to lose any of them. You get close and they make a getaway. That hurts me more than anything. I've had one a few yards away and he'll turn a corner and —whiff!—he's vanished. Gone up in smoke. I don't know where they go."

We go to the precinct house for the evening break, a half-hour mealtime break. It glows with a festive air, as if a party might be in progress. Lights blaze and squad and unmarked cars, many with motors rattling, are double-parked up and down the street. It is an alive outpost through the night—like the depot used to be in Tennessee. The sergeant has a muffin washed down by coffee as his meal. Then he lingers by the front desk, where many officers lounge and look weary in the harsh fluorescent light. Everyone yawns—some behind the back of their hands; others open wide and rub their generous bellies at the same time. Others still work. They are bringing in hookers, one after another. A short, grouchy officer in a full black mustache says, "The captain wants bookings, the captain gets bookings!" He signs in three. A tall black patrolman with a shaven, gleamy head leads in a black woman in a purple pantsuit that reveals the elastic of her panties beneath. The black patrolman is in a good humor.

"Why you pick me, man?" the woman says, stamping her foot in a flimsy, spiked-heel shoe. "Why you get me?"

"Because you done naughty," he says, and tweaks her nose.

One woman is sobbing. She says, "I swear to God, I tell you the gospel truth, I was walking to another place just to see a friend. I just come out in the night air for that!" She is in see-through harem pants and a burgundy brassiere.

The lockup is completely filled. There is so little space that the women are shepherded into a locked walkway that is adjacent to two rows of cells. The cells hold men. The light is stark, and there is a bracing scent of ammonia in the air, the result of the cleaning force forgetting a bottle of the liquid and a prisoner throwing the contents against the four walls. The girls in miniskirts and tight pantsuits and shorts lie back on tables or stand sullenly and exhaustedly. Most wear wigs—deep, metallic black or gold. One fragile-looking blonde props her head up with one hand on a table as she runs the other between her legs from behind, stroking her pudenda beneath plum-colored slacks for the benefit of a couple of officers who approach to check the cells. Her face is young, her expression wise and wicked. One woman is angular, with a heavy, large face and a stubble of beard.

"Hey, po-licemen, make this racket stop down here from them cells. We going crazy. We want sleep!"

The noise is loud and incessant, a steady banging and shrieking. Tony, an officer who is set to retire from the force after tonight's shift, makes an announcement. He is large and balding, a roly-poly man, and he is thirty-eight years old. Cops retire early and take second jobs. "OK, enough racket! You need your sleep! If you don't knock it off, you're going to spend tomorrow here, too. You're not going to be booked. Knock it off. I'm warning you!" His speech is evocative of many rantings I have made to my sons at bedtime. His threats and bellows—like mine —go unheeded.

The night winds down into that still period just before dawn.

An officer in plainclothes comes into the station, taking off his tie, moving as if his legs were weighed down. His eyes are bloodshot. He is off duty and has come from a party. He is going to sleep in the station on a cot and not drive home. It is a perk of the job, having a free place to sleep when off duty and not wanting to go home. Officers on duty near the front desk keep touching their guns, as if reassuring themselves that they are still there. They shift their positions. "What'a these johns see in these women anyhow? Jesus," one says.

"You know what I hear?" a trim, dark-skinned officer with a strong Latin accent says. "There's this one guy likes to have a pin stuck in the end of his dick. He gets a hard-on, the girl sticks a pin in there. That's all she has to do. You figure that one out."

"I heard about this guy who lies under a glass table and pays the girl to take a shit on him."

"Does it hit him?"

"I told you. He's under glass. He's not that dumb."

While the officers ponder this, two men in white overalls and high-top basketball shoes enter and do not stop at the front desk. They keep moving at a fast, purposeful clip toward a closed door. "Hey," Sergeant Cappabianca says. "Where you going?"

"I'm going to check my locker. I'm a janitor, I'm cleanup here, and I wanna make sure no one's been stealing from my locker. People been stealing here."

"You tell me you come in here at five o'clock in the morning to check your locker? Let me see some ID."

"I ain't got any."

"Come back when you got some."

"Is that final?"

"That's final."

The two men wheel and streak out as silently and swiftly as they entered. Cops are used to a wide variety of human behavior. They are suspicious of anyone who wants anything. One cop says, "Of all the cock and bull I've heard today that takes the cake. Checking his goddamned locker. I bet you anything he's got no locker here."

"Hell, no, he's got no locker."

"He's a psycho. He's heard there's lockers back there and he wants to get to them. If he's a janitor, I'm a pink-assed albino."

"Oh, we don't know," the trim officer with the Latin accent cuts in. "How can you say? Nothing's been proved." The men who had entered had had Latin accents, too.

In the last few minutes before dawn the sergeant moves his squad car down side streets. I sense light beginning to break and feel that danger has passed. The sergeant seems to be relaxing somewhat himself but says that some of the hottest trouble often comes just before light, in the very calmest moments. You never can tell. We pass a car that has just been cleaned out by boosters, another squad car stopped, cops talking with the woebegone owner and his party who've just returned to it. The owner holds his head in his hands. Out-of-towners, out on the town, who have left suitcases showing inside the car. We linger at a corner where a muscular black man in T-shirt and cutoff pants leans against a light pole. It is five-thirty. The sergeant stares. Finally the black man turns, not choosing to meet his eyes. "Half of my work is street smarts," the sergeant says. "That guy's a night regular, a real bad ass. He'd be harassing people if I didn't stare him down every now and then. I let him know I'm around."

"What kind of people come out at night?"

"From what I've seen, it's as if somebody just turned a rock over and all these strange people come out. You don't see them in daytime. But here at night they come out."

A burglar alarm rings at a fur warehouse in the garment district. We pull over just as a security guard for the alarm system arrives. The sergeant takes his shotgun. The security guard, a bespectacled, somewhat addled youth, possibly just awakened, trails behind. The sergeant covers the small, compact warehouse the way he did the burglarized apartment on Gramercy Park, pausing before a closed door, opening it quickly. Like in the movies. He glances high and low. There is fur everywhere—racks and racks of gray and brown and black with a sheen. The air is chilly and an air conditioner runs in a steady rattle. The security guard finds the alarm switch and turns it off. The air conditioner sounds louder now and we hear the scrape of the sergeant's shoes and the faint beep of horns on the street. "This is one place I wouldn't want to take my wife," the sergeant says. "You ever see so many furs?"

"There's nobody, is there?" the security guard says.

"There's nobody."

A gray light shows over Manhattan as we step out. And a new cast of characters. Men—some with briefcases—are unlocking car doors. Deliverymen with bread and milk are rushing into buildings. Others in gray work clothes are stepping out slowly with lunch pails in hand. Garbage trucks roll. A man at Twenty-third and Third inexplicably holds a balloon, as if he'd just come from the zoo. It is beginning to drizzle.

Seven

THE SHEET IS IN A BALL. I've pulled it off Lis and myself and hold it against my middle like a football. What was the dream? An old woman stretching back on a desk, thin as a rail, lipstick smudged. I moved her nipples with thumb and forefinger the way you do to open a safe. . . .

They've finally turned down "Men in Bed." Thirty-some-odd articles for them and "Men in Bed" goes down the tubes. After three rewrites. The last desperate suggestions for a rewrite came from a nice woman editor with bloodshot eyes (sleepless ones?) who said "my" men were not loving enough, that I was poking fun at them—that some men might be that way, but there was a whole batch of males out there in Relationland who were loving and supportive and untroubled. Give us the good guys! Oh, poor, dear woman, please let me send you a fine guy, someone who won't mistreat you, send him to you in the flesh! . . . The final turndown arrives from on high, through an underling, and what the magazine seems to want is more on the order of what I gave them originally, something snappy. . . . From May to December: fifteen hundred dollars in a write-off fee. . . .

In my mind at three I write op-ed columns that leave no room for argument. I answer the latest "Hers" column. I speak before large audiences. I carry on imaginary phone conversations, often with people long gone. I see them regularly and get in the last word. I appear regularly on television talk shows. I present my case. I tell my side. I reach millions. . . .

I see myself, God help us, on the Johnny Carson show. I'd rather be hit with a bat than actually watch it, but I can't help putting myself before Johnny in my dreams. . . . He's looking across the desk expectantly at me, waiting for the gems of wisdom to flow. His hair is snow white, and he's rubbing an imaginary speck from beneath his left eye. He's good-humored. I feel as I did on the stage of the old Majestic Theater in Johnson City when I was Mickey Mouse on the "Mickey Mouse Show." I feel giddy. . . .

I start with high good humor—but scholarly, with dignity. I won't trade barbs with Don Rickles. I get a chance to tell everyone who's up at midnight what the view from Grub Street's like. Oh, would I love it! . . . Listen, I want you to know that some of the editors on girlie magazines, the real raunch, were poets and dreamers once and had visions of literature. Heads of houses once sold goods at Macy's or worked as stock boys. Yes! It's not what it seems. . . . I once worked on a magazine where we made up entire battles that never happened in World War II, invented hordes of enemy agents in the KGB who never existed, Chinese torturers who never tortured. The readership swallowed it whole and only sent in letters of complaint when we got an insignia wrong in an illustration. In our last golden days we had a Panzer division mounting attacks on roller skates when fuel was low and being repulsed by a lone Yank in an orange crate on wheels. And we who were putting it out were all writing the most serious novels and plays and poems on the side with truth our only beacon. . . . Oh, Johnny and those up at midnight, what I could tell you.

"I know it's tough out there," Johnny is telling me in my head. And he fiddles with something in his hand. He can't stay still. "Wasn't there something in the *Times*—I forget what exactly"— Johnny getting serious now—"that said writers earn four thousand dollars a year? Something like that. Seems incredible. But that's what it said. How do you manage?"

"I don't know, I really don't. . . . When in doubt I call on the words of Mr. Micawber. I comfort myself by knowing that I can check out Jane Austen from the library, and read Tolstoy and Thackeray once again. George Eliot is so wonderful. I still can eat a Nedick's hot dog at midnight in Times Square and digest it. There are still parts of the world I haven't seen. I swear to you I don't covet a stay at the Beverly Hills Hotel or a week in Vegas nor do I harbor a worry that Elaine will not remember me."

Who am I kidding? Picture hitting an orange ball across a white net on the perfect, cinnamon-colored court behind the Beverly Hills with Alex Olmedo. . . . I want to pull myself from the mire. Wouldn't it be nice to have elbow room enough to take on Causes? Get up there on the podium and speak out against oppression in Poland, the death penalty or something. Get up there like Kurt Vonnegut. I passed him on the street the other day. . . . Or maybe take a Pole and try to get him published. I used to pass Philip Roth in the Village . . . and Edward Albee with his hands held behind him. . . . Or how would you like to spring some guy from the clink? When you're grubbing in the pit, you can't afford the lofty spheres.

Wonder if Christopher Lehmann-Haupt sleeps through the night? Gave me a rave review on my first book. Got the news from my editor at two in the morning. He'd just been out for the papers; I was asleep in my Catskills cabin, convinced no one anywhere at anytime would read or review it. So kind of Christopher Lehmann-Haupt. I hear they call him Chris. Sent him a copy of my second book. Not a peep. I might as well have died after the first one. But who could ever forget that one review, read to me, word for word, over a telephone at two by my editor who had always told me the book would find its way? Thank you, Chris. I hear you play basketball and fish. I got up and poured Jack Daniel's through the night, one belt after another. Jesus, something means something after all. I watched the sun break through the pine trees out front. I went down and reserved a copy of the *Times* at Folkert's in Phoenicia. I couldn't help it; I said, "I've got a review in the *Times* today." The Folkerts are native-born Germans. They speak German among themselves. They didn't quite understand. They run a gun shop and fly rod emporium with Bavarian mugs and cuckoo clocks among other items on the shelves. A review in the *Times?* They did a double take for real the way Carson does for fun.

Mammals got their start on earth by using the night. Cold-blooded reptiles drew in in the dark night as they had been doing for a millennium, unable to function, needing the warmth of the sun to get moving. Platypuses and other marsupials began roaming, feet unstuck, a new breed and order soon to take over on earth. They didn't need the sun; they could work nights. Australia moved from the northern hemisphere down toward the equator. Reptiles began dying out. Mammals evolved into Man. And evolution completed, Man found the day and lives more comfortably there. For most people are larks.

Lorraine is an advanced member of the species. She works in a glamour industry—the media. She trained for it, suffered for it, the way grinds do for medical school. She went through college with a major in "Communications," graduating in 1971, but it wasn't until 1975 that she got a job at ABC. She wouldn't take anything less than the media. Thousands upon thousands wanted the break she finally got—a job in a New York glamour industry. It is wonderful to say you are a Director of a Show. It is wonderful to *feel* that that is what you do. How much better than saying you work as a secretary or a computer programmer. The media steals into every home and psyche. It has pizzazz. It has anchor people behind desks, blasting the news out to the world to the rhythm of the teletype machine. It is important. Reporters stand in front of the White House or near a crime scene, in trench coats, hair windblown, giving us the dope in a low-key, nonaccented voice at any hour. The radio drones in our ears as we drive, and it wakes us in the morning. You have power in the media.

Lorraine is wiry, with a balloon of bushy orange hair. She wears jeans and a plaid blouse and stands in a small soundproof room with thick glass panels on all sides. Every so often a man— an announcer—ambles into an adjacent room of the same size, seats himself, and begins reading the news. He faces Lorraine and looks to her for guidance. She operates a stopwatch and gives him firm, fast commands through an intercom. Her pen flies over copy. She has charge of making sure four news summaries go out smoothly over the air every hour of the night. She works Tuesday through Saturday with Sunday and Monday off. She has few breaks during the night, she never looks out a window, and she mostly passes free time with her plump and jolly female assistant, Cindy, who occupies the same soundproof room. Her schedule seldom varies—into work at eleven, off at six, through the pitch-black dark of night, which she experiences under fluorescent lighting. She has been doing it for five years.

"There are only two good things about working nights for the media," she tells me. "The parking is easier and the pay is good. Regular day people are beginning to pull out of their spaces to go to work when I get downtown around six-thirty. I'm banking money. But people have to be very strong to work nights. I don't eat properly. I haven't eaten properly in five years. My social life is almost nonexistent now. I've had four relationships with men break up because of this night stuff. Just when the evening is getting underway, so to speak, you have to tell him you've got to go to work. It's impossible. All I have is sleep and work. That's it."

"Couldn't you work days?"

"Not if management says nights. Management wants me on nights."

"I've often thought I'd try days," Cindy says sweetly. "I could do this type of work other places. I could—"

"Who asked you, Buttinski? I'm doing the talking now, not you."

Cindy smiles weakly, on the verge of tears. "You got up on the wrong side of the bed this morning."

"This morning? *Tonight* I got up on the wrong side of the bed. *Tonight.* Listen, some people thrive on this type of life. Those are the loners of the world." She hitches her jeans up and shoves her shirttail in. She seems always in motion. "I'm not one of them. I'm never rested. I'm always exhausted."

"Pardon me for asking, but why don't you just quit?"

"How can I? I worked so hard to get into the media. It's such a glamorous field! How can I give it up now and work in some office like everybody else?"

In the ABC-TV newsroom, business goes on twenty-four hours a day. It slows during the late hours usually, a smaller number of bodies around, less hectic, but the pulse of the news beats on. Phones ring. The teletype machines crank away. On the wall are clocks denoting various times with names of cities underneath each one: It's 9:25 in Cairo/Tel Aviv; 10:25 in Moscow. It's now 2:25 in the morning here in New York. Dave Cohen, a director of news, flips around in his swivel chair, passing along quick, sure, arcane judgments into the phone, making notes, glancing at the array of clocks. Absolutely no one watches the four colored TV screens, mounted into the wall, where the current programs of competing networks and ABC play without sound. Tom Wolfe is seated in a chair on one screen, being interviewed. Tom wears a fine-tailored dark jacket, a nifty cravat, and pants creased to razor sharpness. He seems so relaxed and amiable, lips moving without sound, chuckling now, leaning toward the interviewer, legs crossed. . . . He's taped this program earlier—doesn't have to stay up this late himself. Probably making some zzz's right now in his town house. "People wind up where they do best," Dave tells me. "I function best at night."

He's twenty-eight and began his career as a disk jockey on a radio station in South Carolina in 1972. He worked six nights a week down there for $145 a week. He moved around, as media people and repertory actors in England do, to a year in Roanoke, some time in Lynchburg, then Charleston, West Virginia. Always working at night, always restless. He answered ads in a trade publication for TV and radio journeymen. He met his wife-to-be in Charleston when she became taken with his late-night aplomb on television news and petitioned her brother, a policeman and acquaintance of Dave's, to make the introductions. Dave is Jewish, his wife Southern Baptist, and they have no children. His wife converted to Judaism. They live now in Morristown, New Jersey. "This business takes a toll on marriage," he says. "I think if you look around ABC News you'll find a fifty percent divorce rate."

"Does your wife get miffed at your working nights?"

"She understands, but she doesn't accept."

Dave rolls in at home in midmorning by which time his wife is at her daytime job. Often as not he'll have a drink in the bright light, unwind a little, and then climb into bed. He generally does not arise until six in the evening, time to catch the early-evening news, to get a feel for what may be late-breaking stories for him to handle that night. He has dinner with his wife and then drives into Manhattan. He never has to worry about rush-hour traffic. Cops on night duty mention this exuberance at seeing office workers coming in while they're going off—and hotel clerks, cabbies and bartenders do, too. Dave's learned not to split his sleep up, not to have a minislumber then do something and try to catch up with naps. He spreads the word through the neighborhood that he is out during the day, trying to educate friends and those who do business that he is non compos mentis then, *out*. Now and then a paper boy slips through and knocks, a salesman calls. He leaves his phone on the hook, because he can't bear to think of himself as completely cut off from the world. He's in the news business after all. But he suffers from the odd caller, a throaty woman wanting a donation to the Heart Fund or someone making a pitch for Greenlawn Grass.

He's off work Friday and Saturday nights and begins preparation for the holiday by rising early on Friday in order possibly to sleep through that night. The very toughest thing about his schedule, he feels, is turning his sleeping pattern around during the times he is off, then reversing it when he goes back on nights. He fights sleep on Saturday afternoon, wanting to be able to sleep through that night, and his body rebels. It can be all he thinks about of a Saturday afternoon—sleep. On Sunday he catches some shut-eye in the afternoon so that he'll be better prepared for work that night. The cycle then starts all over again.

Dave is certainly awake now at 3 A.M. in the newsroom. He wheels around in his chair, speaks in staccato bursts and seems, even when seated, to be on the move. He tells me that he recently lost a hundred pounds—on purpose. He lost it over a nine-month period, and he is certain being on night work helped. There are not the constant reminders of food during the night shift. There is no expense account lunch—in fact, no lunch. Dave gets an hour off during his night shift, but he seldom spends it eating. In the mornings, when there is light, he often has a huge breakfast with a coterie of others who have been up through the night. There is a certain celebratory air after making it through the dark hours. There is a feeling of camaraderie among those who have done it together. At the

Emerald Tavern on Columbus Avenue they are swigging martinis at ten in the morning.

A young man called Neil, who hunches over a desk in the newsroom, smiling weakly, is not that enthused over night work. He has a soft voice, blond hair, and gentle features. He is twenty-three and has been at ABC for a year and a half. Nights go to the very young who are starting out, to those who have made bosses angry, and to those few who enjoy it. "Nights are not normal," he says, barely managing a chuckle. "I'm always exhausted. I've started working out in this health club right after leaving work in the morning, and that relaxes me and helps me get a better sleep. But nothing really changes the fact that night work is not normal. I'm single, and I hardly have a social life working nights. I'm given Tuesday and Wednesdays off—and I've tried to think of it as a weekend, but no way. On the weekend you get the Sunday *Times.* 'Sixty Minutes' comes on the air. No way is Tuesday and Wednesday the weekend. I'm always exhausted."

Another man, named Eric, lounges back in a chair, legs well apart, chin on his chest, unhappy, with a nervous laugh. The first days of glory for being connected with television have long since passed for him. He is forty-two and black. "About the only positive thing you can say about working nights is that you don't have to see the brass. They're all home in bed and not about to check on you."

His normal routine is to leave the newsroom at nine-thirty in the morning, get home to Mount Vernon by eleven-thirty, eat and get to bed by one in the afternoon. Then he sleeps fitfully until seven or eight when he rises to shower, eat another meal and catch the 10:33 train to New York. "I have no home life except on Saturdays and Sundays."

Outside, it is still along Central Park West. Footsteps click. Up the length and breadth of the street, no one stirs. Now and then a taxi cruises by. From the park, though, suddenly comes a series of whoops and mad giggles as if it were high noon. Somewhere low in the bushes games are being played this moment in the dark. I take a cab downtown to the Village and drop in the Lion's Head. Mike is a few minutes from bolting the door. He has been the night bartender there since before anyone remembers. Come down to the Lion's Head for the very last drink of the evening and Mike will be there to serve you. He has rugged good looks, a model's look, with a full head of perfect white hair. One look at him and you think, Here is someone who should be on a magazine cover or on the screen. He himself thought so for a while. At night he tended bar and during the day made the rounds of casting offices. It never really paid off. He got a commercial once in a great while, but it never equaled all the efforts he put in. Now he just works nights and has forgotten the bright lights. He's put on a little flesh around the middle since I last saw him. He says he is having foot problems from having to stand constantly while he works. No shoes seem to fit quite right. He's caught between hating nights and glorying in it for the money it provides.

"If you're a bartender in the Village and want to make money, you work nights," he says. He moves up and down the bar with a totally deadpan expression, sweeping a drink down, drawing a beer. He doesn't spill a drop. His strong jaw still juts out in profile everytime he rings up a sum on the cash register, as if an invisible casting director might be seated at the bar. But there is a weariness, a slowness I had never noticed in him before.

"Nights are the lousiest," he says. "It fucks up any relationship you have with a woman. It's no life. I get out of this bar at six-thirty. I go back to my apartment and maybe watch a little TV and fall asleep. Used to be I'd eat a big breakfast after leaving here—but no more. That's how you put on a lot of weight."

But he makes good money at night. And one reason he hangs onto it is that he is working while everyone else is celebrating. Nights on the town are no problem. He's got nowhere to throw his money away. He watches the dollar, and makes investments. He has bought land in Rhode Island and an acre in Vermont. Now and then he splurges and goes to Europe on vacation. It's what he has to look forward to. The last time he spent two weeks touring Ireland with some buddies and then a week by himself in Paris. All of this paid by ambling back and forth behind the bar all night long.

Someone is bitching about the Yankees down the bar. Someone is always bitching about baseball at the Lion's Head. There are only four or five die-hards now left at four o'clock. The Lion's Head used to be jammed at this hour back in the seventies. Mike tells me that young people aren't staying out late these days. But ghosts remain in the Lion's Head. I was sitting on this barstool, just the way I am now, foot easily up on a rung, when I watched my future wife walk in—watched her walk in so innocently, carrying a satchel for her work, little knowing (or I knowing) what lay in store for us. The ghost of that moment lingers in the dim light, in the whiffs of salty malt, every time a stool creaks.

This is the place where I used to run into Normand Poirier. Who remembers Normand Poirier? When literary anthologies come out, his work probably will not be there. Literary histories will not include him. I remember him. He was the one who put the Lion's Head on the literary map. He was working for the old New York *Post* back then and led a few drinking cronies to the bar a short time after it opened on Christopher Street. Droves of writers and their groupies mysteriously followed in his wake. Normand had wavy white hair streaked with black, the smooth, velvety voice of a radio announcer and thick spectacles. He was wicked, irresponsible, a womanizer, a fine raconteur, game, sad and about the best companion you could ever hope to find for late-night carousals.

We used to eye one another down the length of the Lion's Head bar before we met—little flickers of the eye, ready to shift the moment caught. We didn't know where to place each other in the literary pecking order. I had more publishing credits, but he had more of a legend and more was expected of him. Those matters were not taken lightly back then at the Lion's Head. When one of us regulars finally put a book between covers, our very first act, after leaving the publisher, was to rip the cover off and paste it to the Lion's Head far wall. Very important. Somehow, after something I had had published, I forget what, I finally passed muster with him. We became fast friends—for about two months. Nearly every evening we would meet at the Lion's Head around nine or ten, have a martini or two, and then amble up to the Bells of Hell on Thirteenth Street, which featured a pool table under a disk of hot white light in back. We formed a partnership and took on all comers in games with small but important wagers. We also got increasingly loaded as the hours slid by. Once a nervous, smiley young man in paint-splattered denim raised his cue over Normand's gray head: "I don't like your shit, man. You say one more cutting word and I'll bop all your brains out. One more word!"

Normand could be caustic. He looked at the fellow owlishly through his thick lenses and began chalking his cue slowly. He wet his lips.

"One word—!" The cue higher in the air.

It was all Normand could do not to utter that one fatal word. It was the only time I saw him quieted. Usually he was passing on literary and culinary judgments mixed with an analysis of all the women he had known through the years. He had known a lot. A few of them I had known also. He loved a story and a drink, preferably together. That night, with the cue rising above his visage, he kept quiet, to talk another time. "I was only afraid that that guy might knock my teeth out," he told me over the next drink. "I saw my caps going. What woman would look at me twice if I didn't have these caps. These caps are all I got left."

We closed up the Bells usually with our drinks paid for with winnings from pool gambling, and then we caught a final big meal at the all-night Pink Tea Cup on Bleecker. We walked down Seventh Avenue past St. Vincent's Hospital, where Dylan Thomas had died, on past the Vanguard, where I had seen Lenny Bruce do one of his last routines—funny and sad at the same time, his hands puffy and his entire act accomplished in a tan raincoat buttoned to the top. Dead within a year. Normand walked like a boulevardier, his feet splayed apart, white head tilted back. We felt we owned New York then—or I should speak for myself. I felt I owned New York. I had a couple of novels under my belt—both respectfully reviewed, both into paper-backs—and a multitude of articles published. I was now in total command, had found my voice, and had a lot more books ready to pop out. Normand had served his time as rewrite man, as a leg man on papers, and had dutifully tried his hand at a book. He had had his problems with booze and busted marriages, but he always came back. He proved he could come back by the way he conquered night now—staying out till dawn with a full head of steam on, still raring to go. He had all the confidence in the world—so it seemed—that he was going to make a comeback. Was going to get a desk job at the *Daily News,* going to tie up with a new woman and get entrée to a new apartment. He was living in a sublet then. So many people back then lived in sublets—particularly those trying for comebacks.

We talked about writers as we strolled down Seventh—Mailer and Hemingway, some of the early *Esquire* crowd, O'Hara and obscure Village writers no one had ever heard of. We quoted poetry. We told each other hair-raising anecdotes about military experiences. He had been in the Navy; I the Army, Korea. No matter what path we took in conversation, a byroad would inevitably lead off into remembrances of women we had lost. Normand had lost many, nearly all remembered fondly. He had lost two women who were sisters, both his lovers. He had lost them simultaneously to each other. He and one sister had contrived to give the other a sleeping potion and pave the way to her corruption. It had worked—too well, for both left him in a glow of Lesbos. He had seduced many married ladies, one atop a trash can, in an alley, after leaving the Lion's Head. The woman immediately left her husband for him. I loved his stories; mine were no match. He was thoroughly without scruples, which made his stories all the more delightful. Some would have called them—and did—despicable. Ditto himself. A woman who heard of my hanging out with Normand said, "How can you do it? He's evil."

I knew. I liked him enormously. We were both caught at this turn in our lives with night on our hands. We had no homes to succor us. Nothing. We couldn't stay still for sleep. We roamed the bars, combed the Village for action and got ourselves through the dark hours. It was a watershed period for me. I had said farewell to a woman right before—a nasty, cantankerous breakup. I was getting older, more tired. Normand looked so tired; one of his blue eyes sagged lower than the other. But we marched into the Pink Tea Cup, boulevardiers. We ordered eggs sunny-side up, a rasher of bacon, a host of home fries, coffee, toast and biscuits, redeye gravy. The Pink Tea Cup was a black-run establishment. Dark faces peered from behind the

counter. Chipper, neatly groomed waiters, like ghosts of Black
Muslims, took orders. Shafts of dawn light often broke into the
Pink Tea Cup as we swallowed the last dregs of coffee and got
set to depart. Even then Normand didn't want to say farewell to
night. He hung back with a copy of the *Times* while I wound my
way toward my sixth-floor walk-up. There were times, though,
when he did shuffle out—looking old, his face lined in the gray
light, coughing his cigarette cough. "See you, buddy," he'd say.

"So long, Normand. See you tonight in the Lion's Head."

He moved in with a recently divorced woman who had a Kips
Bay apartment. He got hired by the *Daily News;* he got fired by
the *Daily News.* He went to work for *Newsday;* he left *Newsday.* He died in St. Vincent's from cirrhosis of the liver. He had
come to New York with all the ambitions any of us had—wanting to write the great book, see the sights. He had had an article
published in *Esquire.* That was where his reputation rested.

. . . I think of Normand as I leave a deserted Lion's Head for
a final snack before bed. He seems beside me as I go to the all-
night diner on Sixth Avenue. But he vanishes as I step in. Other
ghosts haunt the place. I remember going there with Milton
Klonsky after the Corner Bistro closed one night. The Corner
Bistro was where we hung out that season. Milton had sad eyes,
worse eyesight and a gruff, nervous manner. You found he said
very witty things when you listened closely; he said shocking
things, too, like praising Senator Joe McCarthy. He had read
everything. Oh, how I wanted friends those first few months I
was in the Village! I was used to friends, and New York had
strange methods for meeting people. You met them at bars or
parties or on the street. You didn't grow up with them. Maybe
Klonsky could be a buddy, I had thought, the kind of buddy I
was used to back in Tennessee.

Klonsky had his rituals. He did his myopic shopping in Sloan's
supermarket, toting home twin brown bags in two arms. He
liked to pick up a brownie on the sly from Party Cake at Christopher and Greenwich. He dropped in Robby Goldoff's Marloff
Paperback Corner at Sheridan Square to browse. You could
catch him in a movie occasionally by himself, slumped down in
his seat, eating candy like a boy. He briefly had a fling at working out at the McBurney Y on Twenty-third Street. He ran

around the track four or five times and seemed embarrassed doing it. He stayed out late in the Corner Bistro and the No Name Bar down on Hudson. I wondered how he made a living. Someone told me that he picked up spare change editing books for a vanity press.

I was then working as an editor on some lurid men's magazines; I fancied I was in the literary game, like Alfred Kazin. As largess a buddy would dole out, I sent Klonsky some issues of the magazines, featuring hot inside articles on how a nympho brigade stopped Rommel at El Alamein and the lowdown on the rock-around-the-clock dolls of New Orleans. Would he like to contribute and pick up a quick three hundred dollars? Klonsky thanked me with a pained grin and asked that I never say he ever considered writing for such magazines. Of course he never did. He wrote the finest prose—learned and rhythmically pure. It was funny and it was perfect. I marveled when I first read it, a dissertation on "The Flea." All the sacrifices he was making for art, the endless strolls and tortured existence, was to turn out a piece on a flea. But what a wonderful study! He had an article in *Esquire* on Joe "Professor Seagull" Gould and Maxwell Bodenheim. Everything he wrote was so wonderful to read. But no one reads Klonsky except a few of us. There is not a wealthy backlog of Klonsky material. His last effort was in trying to figure out how to get a MacArthur Grant. He died of lung cancer.

. . . Now I see that booth where we had sat over a decade and a half ago at this same late hour. The prevailing atmosphere then, as now, is to give the impression that you are going to order and are not there simply to pee in the toilet. The management must have seen some lulus in its time. As a matter of fact, the management is not that ordinary itself. A high-strung manager in a black bow tie and a soiled, sweaty white polyester shirt keeps checking on everything, mostly giving directions as to who may or may not pee in the toilet. I take a seat at the middle of the counter. He wants me to move three seats over. No reason that I can see to move over to the same exact type of seat —but I sense that you cannot argue with this man. He is crazed on seating arrangements. He directs a stoop-shouldered man in threadbare clothes to sit in a booth, not at the counter. The customer says he does not have money, and the manager miraculously passes over this point. As long as someone is seated properly and not lingering in the toilet, he is satisfied.

I order what I am sure will be easy to fix, something that will be mine in a moment, a grilled cheese and milk. I see past a partition to the kitchen, where an Oriental man in a chef's hat is rattling pots and shaking frying pans. He and the manager have brief, staccato arguments every time they pass. Roast turkey sandwiches and short ribs and cheeseburgers and bowls of soup land on the partition counter and then are whisked around the room. Two hefty women in matching caps and tweed jackets take seats, order and eat and leave. "How's my grilled cheese doing?" I ask the man in the bow tie.

He turns to the kitchen and screams, "I got a grilled cheese working."

"I gotcha," the Oriental in a chef's hat replies.

A man down the counter eyes me. He is in leather but has a rather refined face and demeanor. He drinks coffee, cup after cup. A cop lumbers in from a squad car double-parked outside and grabs an order in a brown bag. He does not pay. Everything seems to be moving in slow motion. There is a gritty, dissatisfied taste in my mouth. The man without money receives a Salisbury steak smothered in onions. This is the perfect place for Klonsky's poor spirit to dwell. Light breaks—and still no grilled cheese.

Eight

I AWAKE coughing in mid-stride, a deep, fruity blast that shakes the dusty framed pictures atop the wall cabinet. I'm reminded that I should stain that cabinet-cum-work-desk. We got it over two years ago unfinished from a cabinetmaker, and it remains as unfinished as the day it was faultily glued together. Lis coughs, and her shoulders twitch up in the air. We cough back and forth, a coughing contest. Then, as leitmotiv, come deep wracking honks from the boys' room. Which one? Both—oh, God. . . .

Let's see, one visit to Dr. Sussman is now twenty smackers, but he'll include both for thirty dollars, like getting the second can of Ajax cleanser for half. . . . Don't forget that insurance will cover 80 percent after the first hundred. . . . But have I been sending in the bills for credit? . . . No. Something keeps me from doing it. . . . I keep losing the receipts. . . . I pitch them on the desk and they go down the Black Hole. . . . Things disappear in this house—manuscripts, a whole supply of ties, coats, shoes, books. . . . They go down the Black Hole. . . . I wouldn't mind going down it myself at times. . . . A whole set of ties; I've been looking for them for two years, all my best ties, my only ties. People wonder why I wear turtleneck sweaters so much. . . . A string of strangled coughs gets me. Whooowheee. It even impresses Lis, who's beating me on the back and coughing herself. . . . I grope on the kitchen shelf for any kind of pharmaceutical bottle. Chances are it will be cough medicine or a cold remedy. Here's one for David, the label showing it's only a year old. Not bad. I take two big gulps and warm my throat. . . .

What work is there out there to be done, to bring in moola? I lay on my side toward the wall, eyes open. . . . Bill Smith pulled off *Gorky Park*. Only in Russia three weeks, and he pulled off a blockbuster. . . . I remember him working at Magazine Management for a hundred a week, a sweet, crooked smile on his face. The nicest guy . . . I could kill him. . . . Gail is going to make a mint on her latest, too. I remember her in London when she worked for a U.S. travel service and wanted to write. Of everyone I've ever met who wanted to write, she wanted to write. She kept on, through a busted marriage, through a bereft New York period, through lost manuscripts and lousy people. She kept persevering. She made her will prevail. She will clear a quarter of a million at the very least. I could kill her. . . . Mario used to have colds when he hustled four-hundred-dollar magazine articles. Very bad colds. Now with $2 million contracts a runny nose and an infected ear aren't enough. He has heart attacks. . . .

I've got it! . . . Think of this. . . . It's Washington and a strange fellow is appearing around town. He crops up like Lon Chaney in different disguises. He's a butler at a diplomatic reception. He's a temporary chauffeur for Ben Bradlee and Sally What's Her. He's a mysterious announcer on Washington's Good Music Station. He's hawking newspapers on Fourteenth Street. He's working as a geriatric counterman for People's Drug. He's a blind man on F Street. He's cracking crabs in Georgetown. . . . Who is this guy? There is something very mysterious going on. Something weird happens after each of his impersonations. Who is this man? It . . . is . . . the President! Why is he slipping out of the White House and putting on disguises and playing parts? That's the hooker. That's why we're writing the book. . . . Keep 'em guessing. . . . It's a thriller and a chiller. . . . Somehow World War III is averted at the last second. Why is he doing it? . . . Because . . . the silly son of a bitch has acting in his blood. He's got to play these parts and put on the greasepaint. . . . I'm going crazy.

Let's see . . . bills go over three thousand dollars. . . . Oh, income tax. I forgot you, income tax. . . . There are ladders you slip down in this business. You reach for the stars . . . and plummet to hell. . . . Think of Henry Z. He used to turn out fast biographies of people who were thrust into the headlines overnight. He really wanted to be a playwright, but failed.

Kennedy got assassinated and pronounced dead at 2:00 EST. At 3:22 Henry got the assignment to do a biography of Lyndon Baines Johnson. While everyone else is glued to the set, watching Oswald arraigned, watching Oswald get plugged by Ruby, weeping over John-John saluting in his little gray cap—Henry Z. is holed up in a one-room Brooklyn Heights bachelor pad, a place reeking of cat pee, tap-tap-tapping on the keyboard, bringing the native of Johnson City, Texas, up to date. Good-bye New Frontier, hello Great Society. In the blinking of an eye . . .

He did the first study of Eichmann. The moment the news flashed out of Latin America that Eichmann was nabbed, no one on the street knowing who the man in thick glasses really was, Henry Z. was rolling a white Hammermill sheet into his Underwood and beginning the first study of the death camp bureaucrat. . . . It may have done something to Henry Z. to be forever connected with disasters and horrors. . . . Or maybe he could be thought of as a casualty himself, one in reverse, for the rash of assassinations was winding down finally. . . . Henry Z. couldn't pay his taxes one year. . . . No money left. But it had been a good life while it had lasted. . . . He would soak up Bourbon and ginger in the 55 Bar, buy one new record each day and coast along for months; then a disaster would strike, and Henry would write steadily for one week, no sleep. Out of one year he would work like a maniac for one week. In one week he would turn out a book which would be reviewed in the New York *Times* as, "One of the first and surely one of the most thorough, etc., etc." . . . Henry Z. was a Kenyon graduate, a student of politics. He never wrote any of the girlie-girlie stuff that some of us have been reduced to. He carried himself like Abraham Lincoln. The IRS broke him like they broke Joe Louis. . . .

Henry Z. started driving a cab. Back in the early seventies he first went behind the wheel of a Checker. He's still there. I guess he is the worst driver I have ever sat beside. Once he drove me to a jazz concert in Connecticut, halfway in second gear. ("What's the matter with this car?" he screamed, unable to pass a truck on a hill. "God, Henry, look. You got it in second. Shift down, man.")

A taxi waits for the writer who can't hack it anymore behind the typewriter. It waits out there like a hearse. Some people can't teach and can't get grants. Poor Henry has been robbed, booted, maimed and stiffed. He drives by night. He's organizing cabbies into a union. He's still very political.

Oh, God, please. Whatever thou doeth—please don't putteth me behind the wheel of a cab. I've been there already. In L.A. Remember, I wrote a book about it. I don't want to die in Harlem, with my face down on the floorboard, a .38 going pap-pap-pap into my temple. . . .

Cockroaches begin to be active just before nightfall. They have been around for eons and have lasted this long by learning to adapt. Night offers the safest haven. Their activity rises to a frenzied peak in the early part of the night and then drops to a low level halfway through the night and remains at that level throughout the following day. No one in New York seems able to shake this nighttime bug. . . .

We called in an Exterminator from the Bronx, a man with a lilting Irish brogue. He sealed off the kitchen and squirted a breath-stifling liquid to the four corners, behind the refrigerator, the drawers, over shelves and along the walls. He said they were gone and good riddance. They in fact lay low for a month and then began to trickle back until they became a regiment. We heard from someone that boric acid would do the job—just lump it in corners and line the baseboards and the roaches would take off. The friend, a city paranoid, said, "Don't tell anyone about it."

We scrubbed and cleaned and dropped the snow-white powder in all the right places. For a while you could blessedly come to the kitchen at eleven at night for water, flick on the light and see no brownish being scurry for a crack. It lasted a year. At first a lone one would be spotted on a midnight cruise or one scouting the terrain before the night shift began. Now large lumps of the white powder abound, and an army of these prehistoric insects are part of the household. Lis is convinced that their internal clocks are set to come to dinner with us. We sit before our butcher block table in the kitchen, bites slowed or stopped while one family member's eyes suddenly becomes fixed on a certain spot on table or wall. "Get him. There he goes!"

We whisper at first in the pathetic belief that the roaches won't hear us that way. Then we bark. We stamp out one or two, and it gives us the sense of not giving up completely, of at least still being in the fight. . . .

My friend Ben was a night-owl composer who barricaded himself in his Upper West Side apartment for months at a stretch with a greyhound to keep him company and cockroaches who roamed, fat and lethargic, and without fear or concern. I once had dinner with him. He was a good cook. Molly the dog skittered through the combo living and dining room on long nails and some of its excrement. She would be reprimanded occasionally by her owner. "Down, you silly old girl! Down!"

Molly would race, in high excitement, and put her paws on me as I tentatively took in some soup. Her nails got caught in my jacket and I had to work them out while she licked my face. And as I listened to Ben tell wonderful anecdotes about Virgil Thomson and Artur Schnabel, I watched cockroaches move up a steam pipe in long, steady lines. They fell from the ceiling like rain. One actually landed in the host's soup, and he deftly swung it out and to the side with his spoon—not commenting. He had given up the battle.

The beaver is another nocturnal animal who will not be erased. He has been around since the Eocene Period, some 55 million years ago. Four feet long and the largest North American rodent, he spends half his life beneath the water's surface and rarely sets foot on dry land. He builds dams in order to have water covering the entrance to his lodge. Predators have a tough time getting to him. They don't see him in the daylight, and at night he moves stealthily on his rounds and uses his sharp incisors to fell trees a foot thick. Valves in his ears and nostrils shut out water as he swims. He lives off roots, shoots, twigs, leaves and the bark of plants. He is a solid citizen. A male and female meet and court and eventually set up housekeeping in a cozy lodge beneath ground and protected by water. They produce two or three offspring each winter and then bring them up. Usually there are around six or seven beavers in a lodge at any one time. After two years a young beaver strikes out on his own and starts his own lodge. Beavers survive in virgin forests in eastern Quebec and side by side with bustling airports. A jogger by Dulles International Airport recently spotted five active beaver dams as a Concorde screamed overhead. Cockroaches and beavers can be called two successful night creatures.

And then there are small animals, such as mice and shrews, who are neither diurnal nor nocturnal but tremendously successful. They have solved the dark/light problem by not paying attention to it. They sleep three hours and are active three hours—right around the clock. The moon and stars mean nothing to them.

Most humans are calling it quits by eleven at night. The news is flicked on, and one nods away during the commercials. At eleven-thirty there is the danger of being snatched by Johnny Carson if one's guard is not up—a "guest" one wouldn't mind watching. No matter who the "guest," he's sure to come on at the very end. The mistake of skimming the TV lineup in the paper may result in your switching over to another channel for an old movie. They're having reruns of "Saturday Night Live" now, and there's a real pitfall. You watch the dancing images from between your parted feet, asking your partner to squirm over a notch if a blanketed bump blocks the view. In the windows of the apartment house across the courtyard the sets are on, images causing shadows to dance on ceilings and floors. I was once stranded on a street in Brooklyn at eleven, and there was no sign of life anywhere. Eerie. Up and down long blocks no one moved. No lights shone in any apartment, any house. No car passed. It was as if a strange nerve gas had settled on Brooklyn, stilling the populace and making it a ghost town. My eyes adjusted after a while and I saw from between slatted blinds that screens flickered within. They weren't entirely dead. Deep in basement rec rooms, away in bedrooms, the sets played on. Across America I envisaged the same scene—rows of dark houses with images jumping on screens inside.

At Bradley's on University Place in New York no TV plays at night. Jazz is played in a minuscule area off the bar and right before what is called the dining room begins. Someone plays the piano and somebody plucks the bass, and there's a saxophonist or whatever it takes to make a jazz ensemble. At the front of the bar, right as you enter, there is a glut of ebullient, eternally youthful-looking people, there for pickups. They look as if deep in their hearts they might be more comfortable back home watching TV. Further back into the smoky dimness of Bradley's are the regulars—there to the end of the night. There is the Stockbroker, as he's called, a man in an argyle sweater and a welter of bonhomie. He calls to say he's coming, I'm told, and they always have his drink ready to place in his hand—a twelve-year-old scotch with soda on the side. There is a slender, shiny-faced man with a full head of snow-white hair. I hear his hair turned white overnight. One evening he spent in Bradley's as a brown-haired individual; the next white-haired. No one knows why. There is a bubbly, dark-haired woman who enters right when things begin grooving in, and she shows the telltale signs of just beginning her day. Her eyes have an early radiance, there is a scent of fresh toothpaste and her movements have a peppy, early-rising quality. It's two in the morning. She makes her living as an agent for jazz musicians, and she table-hops. Jazz musicians who don't have a gig this night, who perhaps are passing through town, drop by and stay to the end. They don't spend much money. Bars do not make any fortunes from jazz musicians.

At the farthest table, by the pay phone, and an ax handle's length from the kitchen, sits himself, Bradley. Bradley is a tall, shambling man with a rose-hued road map of a face, filled with all sorts of curves and pockets. A strong, fleshy, distinct visage. He has the bluest eyes. He was practically the first person I met when I came to New York twenty years ago. I had read about Chumley's from Village lore and went there on one of my first nights to roam. It was supposed to be where Edna St. Vincent Millay had drunk, where the regulars tacked up the jackets of their novels and where there was absolutely no sign out front on Bedford Street that a cozy bar and chophouse lay inside. Bradley had blondish hair back then, carried about thirty pounds less on his body and moved as quickly and deceptively as a cat. He was night bartender.

If a soothsayer had come in that night and said, "Twenty years from now both of you will have a son in kindergarten at the Grace Church School," would we have believed him? I drank through the night on that occasion in Chumley's; one remembers certain nights. I can still see Bradley lifting a glass up to the light and polishing it. He was stone sober. His smile was thin and seemed to cost him something each time. I can see his blue eyes leveling in on a noisome character down the bar, giving him the 86. Bradley has the reputation in the Village of never losing a fight. A mass of flesh creases his forehead in a frown when he gets angry—a cool, dedicated anger, a single-ness of purpose in it that is impressive. It is impressive because most of the crowd in the Village can't work up much ferocity. We have lost the killer instinct, if we ever had it. We'd rather argue the fine philosophical point or worry over our remaining teeth and never take a definite 100 percent stand on anything.

Bradley waded through many nights at Chumley's. I waded through many magazine articles and much highly wrought prose. Bradley likes writers. Somehow he admires and appreci-ates them. He even reads them. But Bradley takes hold of life in a different way than many of us do. He's proven he knows how to make money, to orchestrate a climate where people come, comport themselves in a certain way and leave him with a profit. It takes an artist to do this well. Bradley knows what makes a New York bar tick. He recognizes a certain type of loner, a kind of misplaced eccentric, who will never rise to full potential elsewhere, and gives him a home. This man or woman must leave the confines of his familiar four walls and go some-place. He has money to spend. He needs a second home, a detachable living room. Bradley knows the look of this soul and welcomes him. Other citizens wouldn't be as welcoming. I wouldn't. You wouldn't. It's Bradley's business, the bar business. He went on to bartend at the Corner Bistro and the No Name, and one late afternoon on West Fourth Street we passed and he said, "I'm opening my own bar. It's called the Fifty-five. Drop on down for a drink tonight, will you." He had me figured. The 55 was the first bar he owned. It preceded the more dignified and grand Bradley's.

The 55 Bar in its heyday was unlike any other bar in the city.

At first it had a glazed "55" in white against a blue background hung over its door, like a French address sign; it was stolen. No mark then signified the place. From street level it looked as if a dark swarm of bodies was practicing some magic rite. One actually had to stoop slightly and peer through a barred window to get a glimpse of the below-ground activity. It was a long, narrow room with a kaleidoscopic jukebox at the far end. Rickety stools graced the bar. The linoleum creaked beneath your feet. I walked in the first night Bradley opened the 55, and I spent years of lost nights there before I came to my senses. Bradley didn't deign to serve drinks at his bar; he chose Malcolm as his chief bartender.

Bradley could pick a potential steady customer. He could pick the perfect bartender from the most unlikely candidates. Malcolm was professorially thin, prematurely gray, and had come to Manhattan to be a theatrical producer. He had grown up the son of a psychiatrist and had gone to prep school with Robert Kennedy. Right before Bradley hired him, Malcolm was painting apartments. He had never dealt with the public, could not mix a drink. He was dead broke. Bradley put him behind the bar and said, "It'll come to you. Ask someone if you don't know how to make it." Malcolm forgot to charge people for drinks; now and then he got as drunk as any customer, which is saying a lot. He would become engrossed in conversation at one end of the bar and forget that he had stranded a whole trough load at the other end. As a joke one man called Malcolm on the bar phone from the pay phone at the back to order a drink. Customers sometimes fixed their own.

Malcolm had a wide range of knowledge. He caught the appropriate article in *The New York Review of Books*. He noted the one important article in the *Times*. He kept up with literature and science and the obscure manias of the 55 patrons. He talked the street argot of black entrepreneurs who had discovered the bar. He knew jazz and cheerfully exchanged anecdotes about Bird and Holiday with the musicians who filed past. He had been a gob in World War II and could hold up his end with war stories and forties slang: "Blow it out your barracks bag, Mac," and "Take five." He had an abiding interest in medicine and psychiatric lore and could diagnose as well as anyone the multiple ailments that presented themselves from across the bar. He once correctly spotted one of my complaints as conjunctivitis. Malcolm was the spirit of wonderful nights spent in the 55 during the sixties and seventies—two hefty, shattering decades. He was in a sense the theatrical producer he had set out to be: Bradley the bankrolling angel.

What happened on the street or world outside had a way of not touching the 55. The place marched to its own drummer. The great homosexual uprising next door, at the Stonewall, went unnoticed. The eventual peacock parade of homosexuals up and down Christopher Street, past our bar's physical location, did not affect the climate of the establishment one iota. A few custom-busting homosexuals, now called gays, dropped in to make sure they weren't being discriminated against by the 55. They were finely dressed and had good teeth. They were served and listened to, but it wasn't their sexuality that eventually counted them out and made them move on, it was their ebullient sense of mission and good humor. They didn't fit in. The 55 succored the doubter, the disgruntled, the often broken, the distinct, solitary dropout—never the one whose time had arrived to shake the world.

Jason was black and homosexual and had seen about everything, and he found nightly lodging at the 55. Shirley Clarke made a documentary about Jason—called simply *Jason*. It could be said to be the high-water mark of his career. He did a little maid's work in the apartments of the more affluent patrons of the bar for pocket change, collected what benefits he could from the government and survived. He wore thick-lensed glasses, had a hangdog look and was about as funny a man as I ever met. He often wore a beret. He cadged drinks by running errands for Malcolm.

Frank, from the South, was another favorite of mine. He was a backwoodsman who had materialized via a Greyhound bus in New York one day to be an actor, and had immediately found the 55. He had a disastrous love affair, couldn't hold a job and began sinking. People stood him drinks and listened to his tales of the South and his quest for acting roles. Then one day he got hit by a car, and his fortunes changed. All for the better. He collected a good-sized insurance award, enough to stay off creditors and allow him to visit casting offices, at first on crutches. He miraculously landed a few parts. He regaled us all, a wide grin spreading, with accounts of the good fortune that had knocked him forty feet.

Frank C. was not so lucky. He had come to New York in beautiful cashmere sweaters, scruffed brown bucks and a tremendous yen to make a name for himself, somehow, someway. He was a movie critic briefly on a small neighborhood paper—his pay, free admission to screenings. He comported himself at these screenings like the town's first-line critic, a George Jean Nathan. He was not shy. He strode in, making comments that caused all heads to swivel. He liked celebrities. His warmth came from reflected glow. He worked and organized many galas and benefits—and never got paid. He staged Norman Mailer's Fiftieth Birthday Bash. He loved writing; he didn't write much. He tried to peddle screenplays and treatments and never had one bit of luck, not one sale in five or six years. He did, however, sell an article of mine to a movie producer. Out of the goodness of his heart, he just up and sold an option on it for five hundred dollars. I bought him the meal of his choice, a Mexican sinus-cleaner with free-flowing beer that didn't end till morning. The movie, of course, was never made.

Frank began to show signs of a disfiguring skin disease, mean red blotches that crept over his body. He was a fastidious man and good-looking, and the disease began spreading over him like a fungus. He took to wearing surgical gloves to hide the damage. We clinked glasses late at night at the 55, and his hand came up, like Dr. Strangelove's, sheathed in the translucent white of a condom. It was always a peculiar appendage to shake. And one wondered how Frank got by. He could have bankrupted his father; he never sponged on friends. He took uptown trips to Elaine's, but his heart remained in the Village. We discussed all new writers, all breakthroughs in prose, and paid respects to the masters who had gone before us.

Frank gradually went downhill, past where I was then able to reach him. I can picture him now in the far reaches of the 55, down by the jukebox, where the black and more seriously out of it lingered. He is drinking and he appears to be in shock. He came to New York, and New York did something terrible to him.

One night he swallowed a mouthful of sleeping pills, stretched himself out on his bachelor's bed, crossed his hands and died. He had written to some select people—Norman Mailer being one—saying that it had been a good fight, but he was checking out. He asked for the word to go out for one and all to belly up to the bar and have one on him. Services were held in a tiny mortuary off Lexington, in the 13th Precinct. His coffin was wrapped in the American flag, because Frank had once been a Marine. Mailer traveled a great distance to be there and say the eulogy. He compared Frank to Jay Gatsby.

I myself did not know what had hit me when I came to New York either. It was a discordant, nervous place that never went to sleep. I loved it; I didn't know exactly how I had made it there, how I was going to survive or what to do next, but I loved it. Just to have got a toehold after traveling a circuitous route from Tennessee was enough for me. I'd let a higher power choose what to do next with me. I answered two ads in the *Times*. One got me a one-and-a-half-room apartment on Tenth Street, the other got me an editor's job on a string of adventure magazines, which was published by an outfit called Magazine Management. Other ads could have dropped me on the West Side and had me toiling on Wall Street. I thanked fate. I soon moved up in the world, to a sixth-floor walk-up on Waverly Place, a roomy, sun-drenched spot except when the drapes were drawn, which was frequently. I quit editing and began free-lancing with the sure, sweet knowledge that one day I would leave a legacy of succinct and true and funny novels. Meanwhile, the 55.

Outside, calm prevailed on the street. Snow fell or humidity settled and pedestrians passed, nothing much to stop for, only a flight of stairs next door to dawdle on. Inside, it was a pirate's den. Grog sloshed and curses sounded. At two in the morning it could be bedlam—the bartender down for the count, customers pouring their own drinks, smoke rife, visibility near zero. Some never left or found their way out till dawn. It was made for the night. Johnny G. was a regular, every night, seven days a week. No one ever discovered how he was able to hold a day job as a highly promising writer for a news magazine. And I never quite got the knack of remembering to take the phone off the hook at night. Somewhere in the heart of night its ring would shake me from deep sleep. "Mr. B., rise and shine," the voice would bark over the receiver, a blast of wild jukebox fare in the background.

"Mr. G. What the hell time is it?"

"Just getting going. I'm down at the Fifty-five. Get your ass down here right away."

"Are you insane? I'm trying to catch some sleep. I got an assignment to turn in tomorrow."

"At ease. Listen, hurry. A bunch of Swedish stewardesses just drifted in here. They can't speak much English, and somebody else is going to land them if you don't hurry. So, hurry!"

No matter how many times it happened, with sundry variations on the theme, I never learned. I hunched my shoulders, strode into the 55 with a put-on look of insouciance, but with a heart of hope and trust, and heard Johnny G. say, *"They just left!"*

Which left the rest of the night to carouse through, the usual ladies of the 55 to knock back a few with. Two women had scars across their wrists from suicide attempts. One old lady was a carry-over from the bar that had been there before Bradley took over, a sleepy, dreary oasis with few clients, a pale, sickly bartender and a working-class aura. (Way back the 55 had actually been a speakeasy.) The old lady wore a pillbox hat with glass fruit pinned to its front. She had a round face, red cheeks and heavy black health shoes. Her feet didn't reach the floor from the stool where she sat. She drank martinis and didn't seem aware that the bar had ever changed owners and clientele. She sloshed her way through the night, calling for long-ago numbers to be played on the juke and muttering to herself.

Now and then a new face showed up. Once it was miraculously a stripper and go-go dancer from Florida, hobbling in on crutches, her leg broken and encased to the thigh in plaster of Paris. She drank Bourbon and ginger and slung ice from her drink when irritated, the glass itself when infuriated. She lived with a man so emphatically sleazy and without principal, a rascal in baggy trousers and Hawaiian sport shirts, that one knew instinctively never, no matter what, to trust him. Yet he had to make his living as a con artist, God knows how. He

roamed around the bar saying "Suckadicksay, *hunh"* to strange
women and goosing old acquaintances.

Delmore Schwartz was there through the last of his nights.
He was near insanity, if not already there. When Malcolm introduced me to a bloated, bulging-eyed man, with a constant tic
that caused a snort to erupt from his nasal passages, and said,
"This is Delmore Schwartz," I thought it was a put-on. He was
making fun of some poor devil, which wasn't Malcolm's style.
He could have said, "This is Dean Acheson," and I wouldn't
have been more incredulous. Delmore had written "In Dreams
Begin Responsibilities"; he was a genius. He was what literature
was all about. He should be at the Harvard Club. But it was
Delmore Schwartz. He died a few weeks later in the depth of
night in a fleabag on Times Square. The 55 had been his last
watering hole.

David Burnett passed through. His mother was Martha Foley
and his father Whit Burnett, who had started *Story* magazine.
David wore a scarf like the French—an end thrown back over
his shoulder. He had terrible teeth and long, lank blond hair.
His body took gargantuan assaults from all the chemicals that he
constantly fed it, and he floated about in a sort of misty perennial high. Yet the barrage of chemicals—cognac being only a
minor one—did not impede his reading nearly everything ever
written or making love to an endless parade of women. I once
asked one of his ex-wives what David had in the amorous department that other men didn't have.

"He is the most sensuous man I ever met," she said.

"Why aren't you still together then?"

"David's women never really ever leave him."

He had a sweetness and sad vulnerability. Maybe he felt
slightly wounded by having to help his mother put out the
Martha Foley collection of best stories year after year. It seemed
his only occupation. He was nice to me when my own first book
came out and its cover was Scotch-taped to the barroom mirror.
Covers went up at the 55 as a joke on the world of Sardi's and
Elaine's and show business success. (Later the cover-hanging
practice was taken seriously by the Lion's Head next door.) The
books never made it to the best-seller lists and never were
intended to reach there. Like the patrons of the bar, the books

carried fatal flaws of being dedicatedly and wholeheartedly out of the mainstream. David applauded this stance and lived his life as an example. He died late at night in the place with his head on the back table, one too many chemicals in him, an open eye blindly staring off past the jukebox.

Johnny G. howled through the night, thirst unquenchable. Never was he still in the 55. Strangely he was calm outside the place. He ordered milk with his meals and talked softly the times we dined out in the world. Inside, he trod up and down the length of the bar, insulting friend and foe. He fought people he suspected of having designs on his girl friend, Big Diane. He often slugged her too. She kept up with him, drink for drink, until dawn, a large hulk of a midwestern woman with a beret to hold back a sweep of blond hair. Outside, in daylight, she was soft-spoken and witty. She wrote highly literate, amusing prose. Johnny G. looked like the young Oscar Wilde, dark curls dangling, eyes large and merry, an affected manner of supreme disdain. He hated all Turks, and got around to the subject sometime during every drinking night. His father was an Armenian, a man who had carved out a good life for himself and his family as a rug merchant in the heart of the Midwest. As a young boy the father had only escaped massacre from the Turks by being dressed as a girl and slipping across borders and finally into America; other members of his Armenian family hadn't been so lucky. They died. In America he had married a WASP, and Johnny G. was their only child. Johnny G. had gone to a top Ivy League college on a scholarship and had edited the campus newspaper. He came to New York to be a writer. The first time I met him I was interviewing some junkies in a restaurant and he was at the same table. I thought he was included in their number, that he had a monkey on his back. After talking to him for a while, it came to me that he was a reporter, too, there to do a story. The next time we ran into each other was naturally at the 55.

There were fights in the 55 that didn't include Johnny G. Three Feathers swung his fists left and right at every imagined and real insult to the Indian nation. Three Feathers came from Oklahoma—as did a wide range of his drinking buddies. All Indians, all in a cluster at the 55 in New York City. They started off evenings quietly, eventually sounded war whoops and then wielded bottles, chairs and tables. They were impossible to cut off at the pass.

I once watched Red, a light-skinned black guy, grab the hair of a white woman and keep her prisoner in the back alcove for an hour, insulting and menacing her. Every time she tried to escape, he yanked her hair and called her "cunt." Every time a nonblack would make a motion to intercede, a formidable black man or two would hiss, "You stay out of this." Red finally twisted the arm of the woman behind her and walked her out of the bar and into the night. His last words that evening in the bar, said over his shoulder, in sudden good humor, were, "Oh, man, it's tough being a nigger."

He came back the next afternoon and apologized, said he had taken the wrong pill. The woman, an actress, never mentioned the incident afterward. It was as if it hadn't happened. She came from Kentucky.

We all brought our pasts to the 55. When Johnny G.'s father began his slow, sure descent to the grave, Johnny G. talked more about the Turkish massacre of the Armenians—if that was possible. He recounted the gentleness of his father, his firm but fair decisions, his courtliness and stability. Johnny G. was torn between his love and sympathy for an exotic father plunked down in the heart of Mid-America, and trying to make accommodation for his mother's side of his family, the WASPs of long lineage in this country. His mother didn't come out too well in the reckoning. Too controlling, too demanding and neurotic and out of control, like Johnny G. himself. Johnny G. was more than a bit of a misogynist. Yet women invariably found him attractive. They thought him cuddly, in need of mothering, interesting, whatever. They stood up for him and called him sweet.

At the 55's official closing hour of 4 A.M., a few of us often struck out for other outposts of the dwindling night. There was a gay after-hours bar in a commodious basement on Tenth Street. All you had to do was be sober enough to identify a certain row of tin garbage cans, pick your way down a dark narrow flight of concrete steps, pass muster before a lad in black leather and then enter a cavernous layout cloudy to near invisibility with tobacco smoke, through which, after a while, you could make out a horseshoe-shaped bar with bartenders furiously laboring and booths at which male couples sat spooning. There was a dance floor, and the latest, sauciest hits bellowed over the airways.

Johnny G. and I entered with women beside us—the ubiquitous Big Diane, hand already out for a drink, and someone who had latched onto my arm in the 55 at the last moment. There was not one window in the gay joint, not one fire exit. A hovering fear of mine was that a fatal fireball might whoosh through, leaving us all a pile of roasts. On the front page of the *Daily News* would be my name among the casualties, and the implication for history would be: queer as a goose all along. What about that? It didn't stop me from enormously enjoying myself there. The gays were polite—a term hardly applicable to the regulars at the 55. We all smiled at each other. Once in a while a fight broke out, but it always seemed more a simulation of a fight than a fight itself, certainly nothing on the order of Three Feathers with a barstool raised above his head. I remember a man in a motorcyclist's studded jacket and cap, a fierce-looking dude, tearing after a stocky youth in a T-shirt, both soon swinging fists but not seeming to hurt each other much. The Hell's Angel's words didn't go with his screeching voice: "Lemme at him! I'll kill the son of a bitch!" But it took nothing to hold him back.

Men danced. They held hands. Some kissed each other. There I'd be, raising a can of Shaefer's, and two clean-cut men beside me would suddenly embrace and begin tonguing one another. Of course, there are far wilder clubs of the night in New York, the hand of the Mafia in most of them. There are cockfights in Spanish Harlem and gambling casinos all over. Money talks in New York, corruption abides, and you learn these facts early.

Even after-hours bars finally close—and Johnny G. and our ensemble wound its way finally out of the subterranean lair. One minute it was foggy and dark and men were kissing and hugging—the next moment there was fierce, brutal sunlight and freshly showered and breakfasted men with briefcases were going down the street to work. Not every night did I stay out till dawn, but plenty. I had another life of sorts. I traveled to Paris and London, Hollywood and Lynchburg, Virginia, on stories, and I barricaded myself when I was back in New York and wrote them up, never taking longer than a week. I bounced between a monkish daily routine and Rabelaisian nights. There was no Mr. In-Between. Once I spent a winter at Yaddo, going to bed at ten, rising at seven, working the livelong day. Wrote a novel. I returned to New York on George Washington's birthday and the 55 drew me to it like a magnet. I hardly had time to unpack. I walked in at two in the afternoon, catching Malcolm having his ritual turkey sandwich from the Gallery Delicatessen, and I did not leave till 4 A.M. I ordered out for food. Somehow at dawn I made it up the marbled stairs of my sixth-floor walk-up. Some nights you don't remember the fine print. I don't remember unlocking the door and getting in or even leaving the 55. I do remember waking in a bath of light, not knowing where I was, and witnessing the biggest, fattest, blackest woman I'd ever seen turn toward me. "Mornin', sugar," she said. She turned out to be good-natured and intelligent. Her Afro glinting like coal in the sunlight, she told me of her failed marriage to a German in Germany. She bitched about some Greeks at whose restaurant she worked. She drank Instant Maxwell House and left.

My mother was struck by a pickup truck in Tennessee as she walked to town one April day to go to the grocery store. She lay in a coma in the hospital. I got the news in the afternoon and made reservations on the earliest flight down, which was the next morning, on Piedmont Airlines. My mother had taught school as a young girl, not much older than her students. She had walked many miles between the one-room schoolhouse and the boardinghouse where she stayed. She was hungry most of the time, she had told me, subsisting on a small cut of country ham between a hard biscuit for her midday meal. She later had, with my aunt who lived with us, the largest private library in eastern Tennessee. She read everything. She had given me a typewriter when I was thirteen, a Noiseless Underwood Portable with a distinct smell that never left it after decades. She paid to have me taught typing at the business college in town, and then I taught her what I had learned. She went back to work and ran a successful bookshop in Johnson City after her last child, me, was set free in the world.

She was hurrying to town to shop early so she could garden in the afternoon when she cautiously crossed the street with the light and the pickup truck cut the corner quickly and hit her. My aunt gave me the message over the phone, her voice different from any time I remember in my life.

I immediately buried the information, froze my mind—for underneath I knew something momentous without recovery, had happened. I poured several Bourbons and ginger ale. I turned on the TV and looked with glazed eyes at whatever was on the screen. I ate a roast pork sandwich out of its paper wrapper from Angelo's across the street, dumbly, slowly chewing and keeping my eyes on the TV screen but not seeing it. The brain surgeon called from Tennessee, someone I had gone to school with. He had been manager of the basketball team I was on in high school and we were fraternity brothers from college. He did not have anything cheery to say about old times. He said her chances were not good. It was past ten o'clock at night. I went to the 55.

The jukebox was blaring, a double row of people stood at the bar, and so many people were laughing and hooting. I had a few drinks and struck up a conversation with a brown-haired woman, a college-student type, someone wholesome-looking by 55 standards. Her name was Ann. She told me she lived with a Hungarian and that one of her main aims in life was to go to an orgy. She had been looking for one since she came to New York but had never found it. She wondered how she would react. She worried a little that she might be embarrassed by her body, but she was keeping in as good shape as possible for when magic did strike. I watched the jukebox playing normally, the usual chatter from blacks in the alcove, the nightly surge in and out of the front door. Time passed. Ann, the brown-haired woman, said the Hungarian was not possessive or jealous. She gave me her number but said to call only between certain well-defined hours. In a daze I tucked her number in my wallet and immediately lost it. I told her how much I loved my mother. Malcolm was tending bar when I entered, but someone else had taken over when I left. . . .

Johnny G. had gone back to the Midwest to look after his mother and fight with her, his father dead. He came back but once or twice, having lost about a hundred pounds. His clothes hadn't been taken in and fell from his skeletal body like a dismantled tent. He wasn't writing anymore, he told me, he was just looking after his mother who kept marrying different men for brief periods.

I flew down to Tennessee to be with my mother. The house at 203 West Watauga seemed itself aware of the accident. That was how we referred to the calamity—the "accident." The house was well-scrubbed and neat, kept that way by my aunt because of the many friends and relatives now passing to and fro inside. They brought food—marvelous, endless dishes. They sat on the edge of the sofa for short, intense moments, people I hadn't seen or considered for ages, eyes moist with pleasant smiles. On the dining table lay hard biscuits under Pyrex glass, one of the last items my mother had cooked. Shoes she had recently used for gardening were in the side hall. A message she had scribbled a day or two before was on the telephone book. She had expected life to continue as before, had had no inkling the light was set to disappear.

I went to her hourly in the intensive care unit for the alloted ten-minute visit. It was May in Tennessee—the days fierce with sunlight, the nights balmy. My mother lay quietly, as if taking a nap, on the hospital bed. There was no mark on her. The back of her head had hit the street after the truck struck her. Around my mother lay the nearly dead—heart attack victims, a teenage girl who'd received a shotgun blast, the mangled from car wrecks. Tubes went into bodies, machines gurgled and beeped. The light had the dull radiance of a fish tank. My brother rushed in and picked out the wrong woman at first, began consoling her until the woman's relatives stopped him. I tried my best to bring my mother back: "Mother, it's John," I yelled. "Please, come on, wake up. Just open your eyes. Please, Mom!"

Visit after visit after visit. The nurses combed her hair and washed her face—but she did not wake. I held her hand. I slept in her bed at home at night because a relative had snagged my old one. The sheets still held her fragrance. Occasionally in the hospital my mother thrashed about, shaking her head, frowning, clutching the sheets. Nurses said she was having dreams. To me it was her spirit fighting to break free, to leave her, to go elsewhere. I had lost my Baptist religion, but that's what I thought. I wanted her to fight back, to hold her spirit in. "Don't let go, Mom! Hold on. It's John!"

Once I was sitting beside her, saying nothing, resigned to accepting fate. She opened one eye and looked directly at me. There was no expression on her face. I jumped up, I began talking again. She was awake! The eye slowly closed.

At home I caught my father reading the Bible, the first time I had ever seen him doing so. My brother had red-rimmed eyes. My aunt stoically fixed meals and got things done. Passing time in the hospital, standing in a bustling corridor, I thought of other moments with my mother: the picnic she arranged for just the two of us when I was three and when I learned what it was to love; all the times she had laughed at some pomposity or ridiculousness in town; the way she had taken my hand and brought me to the first grade, the dictionary she gave me as a high school graduation gift. They put her on the operating table for some kind of neurological test, tapped her spine and took X rays. I had to sign a legal document for them to do it. She was wheeled back into the intensive care unit looking dead—frozen and stiff. I put my hand on the bed for support. The world swam. "Don't go, Mother! Hang on!"

A man with a stubble of beard, lying in the next bed, a coronary, said, "You love your mother, don't you, son?"

"Yes, sir, I do."

But I had given up. After all the yelling and cajoling, after three weeks of buttonholing every doctor I could—I thought it was all over. I had seen a little bit of her spirit ebb away each day until the fight was nearly ended. It was just a question of hours. It would be liberating in a way to have it over. Then at dawn my brother, who'd just come from the hospital, woke the house up. "She's back to normal! Her pulse, everything—it's stabilized and back to normal! It's the most amazing thing I've ever seen."

I went back to the hourly visits, the yelling and the cajoling. I could see no end. Her spirit would not leave. I took off for a day in New York. My brother called me at four in the morning. His voice had a new calm and dignified tone. "We just heard. Mother died."

The house sparkled when I returned. There was a book which people signed who visited in mourning. The undertaker, a nice young man, was appropriately solemn and getting things moving. My mother's clothes and possessions were being divided and taken from their familiar places. I went to the funeral home where her body lay in an open coffin. The light was dim, everything hushed. There was a heavy scent of flowers. I understood fully the meaning of the phrase "passed away." The body was like a replica of my mother—not my mother who had recently lain in the hospital bed. I took her hand and it was cold. Her spirit had left.

Nine

SOMEONE IS CRYING—not one of the boys, thank goodness. It comes from the air shaft, from one of the apartments that face it. A soft, steady moan and whimper. It's a long-suffering, endless grief. It's a woman—or is it? You get on the elevator in the day and everyone smiles and nods—people off to work or Balducci's or a trot around Washington Square; people dressed and purposeful and sunny as hell—but someone cries in the night. You see all of these people at the co-op meetings. They argue and pay attention and take a glass of cool water. Now one of them is sobbing.

I work a leg out from under the cover. I like to keep a bare leg out from under the covers. I read once that Sigmund Freud liked to sleep that way, too. My head is filled with a world of such aimless facts and images. . . . Name another. . . . OK, I once rested my folded arms on Eleanor Roosevelt's behind as she bent over. Can you top that? It was in Johnson City long ago and she was coming through to make a speech in the John Sevier Hotel Ballroom. She had just got off the train and a crowd was milling around. I was little then and I dodged my way through. She leaned over for . . . luggage? Maybe in the golden past First Ladies saw to their own baggage. Everyone was crowding around, and I just folded my arms and leaned against her rump, I don't know exactly why. To be able to remember it some forty-odd years later in New York City? She had on stiff women's stays under a grayish silk dress. The sun was glaring. I can see it all as if a moment ago. She looked a lot like my Aunt Carolyn and was as tall. So much one brain holds. . . . More than all books put together, I bet.

"Daddy." A head comes just over the bed.

I keep my eyes closed and try rhythmic breathing. Lis's breathing is deeper and more profound. We're competing to show who's more thoroughly asleep. It wouldn't be fair to feign a snore—deep breathing, yes; a snore, cheating. I'll take care of him. "What's the matter?"

"Can you come to bedwidme?"

He is wearing his pair of blue-striped pajamas. "David, you know that you have your bed and we have ours. You're too old to keep doing this. You must go in your room now and lie down and go to sleep like a good boy. I'm going to stay here."

An ear-splitting scream, and he's banging his head on the floor. The sobbing from the unknown apartment stops abruptly.

"David," I say, lying now on the floor by his bed, the breeze from the window chilling my bare feet, my lower back sending signals that I've lain on a checker and a marble. "I'm only going to stay with you for a minute. Now close your eyes and go to sleep."

"Talk to me first."

"What about?"

"Dinosaurs, God and outer space."

"Only one of those, David. Then sleep."

"OK, God."

"Well, what would you like to know about God?"

"God just had one boy, didn't he?"

"Yes, Christians think so."

"What happened to God's other boys? Do you think a thief got them?"

"He sent his only begotten son to—He sent Jesus to save mankind. You see—"

"But God just had one boy, right?"

"Yes, God had just one boy."

"And I've got two bloods in me. Right, Daddy?"

"Yes, David, from my side and your mother's."

I work my hand away from the clutch of his fingers. He's down at last. I stand and cover Nick in the top bunk. He has a leg over the restraining board and his arms are every which way, his head at an angle, on his back. He has a definite cast to his face that I've often seen on the Swaffords and Edgemons, my mother's people. I watch him other times from the back and he has the neat, round head of a Shabecoff, from his mother. All of his explosiveness we blame on each other's side. He had a great-grandfather who escaped from czarist Russia and ended up in an idyllic small town in New England; on the other side he had one who fought in the Battle of Chickamauga as a boy, helped a surgeon cut off arms and legs on the battlefield and from what he had learned went home to a farm in Tennessee and began practicing medicine. He had another great-grandfather who ran away from Rumania as a boy, traveled the world and became a bakery owner in New York. He ate a whole onion and took a belt of schnapps each day at lunch. He has a line of Viennese relatives and those who have plowed dirt and taught school in Tennessee for generations. Each person who walks the earth is a miracle. I climb back in bed.

A few years ago there had been no babies. Our last free afternoon Lis and I had shopped for a rug—carefree, in and out of Bloomie's like gadflies from the *New York* magazine world, down to Design Research—and then debated whether or not to have a drink at the Plaza. "Wouldn't it be nice to tell our child we had a drink there just before he or she was born?" We didn't. We wanted to be home before dark.

That night she felt contractions. There had been false signals before, so we thought we might be able to sleep through the night. Put it off—let everything happen at a more convenient time. The contractions increased, with less time between them. I kept time with my father's old railroad watch. Finally they were too regular and strong to ignore. It was one o'clock in the morning. I called the doctor and we prepared to leave for the hospital. We had a pillow, talcum powder, a configuration for Lis to gaze at during the Lamaze ritual and a couple of peanut butter sandwiches. It was all passing as if in a dream—but with a decided feeling that something really momentous was right around the bend.

The taxi driver was anxiety-ridden, a man with lugubrious eyes and a slack jaw. He may have been crazy. He argued over what was the best route for getting one into the admitting room of New York University Hospital on First Avenue. We had planned the voyage for months, had the directions down by heart, but he knew better. "You're crazy, we can't drive right up to the emergency room," he said. "You gotta go in the front way." Swiveling his head, screaming, he ran over the curb and narrowly missed ramming the emergency room wall. But we made it safely.

Lis was taken to the labor room in a wheelchair although she could easily walk. We laughed along the way, ha ha ha, one of our last laughs for a while. We were assigned a room that looked out over the East River, where a soft fog floated around shore lights. A Pepsi-Cola sign twinkled through the mist. A faint foghorn sounded. To one side of us, in a darkened room, a woman lay with the fetal monitor showing a straight green line —no movement. We learned that quadruplets had been inside her and had died before delivery; she had been on fertility pills. On the other side, door shut, a woman screamed. "Oh, God—I can't take it! Help me, help me!" There came much softer, muffled talk from her husband and doctor.

Lis was checked over and prepared for what awaited her by young residents and interns and nurses. She lay back on the hospital bed, her head slightly raised, the fetal monitor attached, the baby's heart beating thump-thump-thump. The contractions were coming closer together now. The pain was increasing on Lis's face.

We began going through the Lamaze method as if required by law. After all, we had taken a class in it and had been practicing the exercises religiously at home for a month. We knew nothing else about having babies. "Contraction BEGINS," I shouted, beginning the count. "PEAK . . . it's coming down, honey . . . breathe deeply. Contraction ENDS!" I felt like a fool, and I wore a baggy blue hospital gown. My mother had delivered me at home in Tennessee on an iron framed bed still in the family—no anesthetic or father pacing nervously in a hospital corridor and seeing the baby the first time through plate glass. He had been right there—as I was now.

Before too long our Lamaze method readjusted itself. Lis was pulling her hair, writhing, and I was doing rhythmic deep breathing myself. I was also cussing the doctor. Where the hell was he? Sweet-natured Indian residents and cooing, efficient black nurses took pulses and blood pressure and moved monitors and wiped Lis's brow and finally gave her an epidural that didn't quite take. The world spun. I held onto her hand and coaxed her toward I knew not what. "Hold on, honey. You can do it!"

When no one was looking, I ate a peanut butter sandwich. I thought of Tennessee and other times and watched the Pepsi-Cola sign blink toward dawn. Lis fought and held on and kept asking where the doctor was and when the pain would go away. Her lips were dry. In the gray morning light the doctor arrived. He himself was going through alimony horrors and fighting child custody decrees and his mood was not the best and his mind tended to wander. I was never so happy to see anyone in my life.

Everything speeded up, and then the doctor took one last examination, smiled and said, "OK, let's wheel her into the delivery room. We're going to give her a baby."

I struggled to get on the required hospital slippers in time, a cap over my head and a mask over my face. Lis was being wheeled in on the double. I saw her look over her shoulder at me as I struggled to get some regulation paper contraptions over my shoes. I almost ran into the wrong room, found the right one, and there Lis was lying back in the stirrups. The doctor was seated before her—like a pilot about to bring in an airship. Everything was hushed, dramatic now. The light was blinding. Lis reached for my hand. She took an Indian doctor's by mistake and called him "darling." He smiled sweetly. "PUSH! Come on now, honey—PUSH!"

It could be that every moment of my life was a preparation for this one. The baby came out swiftly, almost running already. He was held up by his feet, blood and mucus dripping and him wailing—a beautiful little baby. I saw his penis. Next I heard: "It's a boy!" I was wiping away the tears.

Bradley tells me that he has stopped going to the 55. He owns it, but he doesn't darken its door. It seems somehow to run itself. Bradley looms through the night here at Bradley's at his back table. He chain-smokes, but he is not drinking. I remember how he used to put away orange juice and vodka in a couple of gulps, ice and all. Jazz buffs stop and pay him court. The musicians bum his cigarettes. He passes on a word or two of wit to each visitor and the effort seems painful. He doesn't rise from the table unless he has to. The jukebox goes dead between sets and he lumbers down to fiddle with it to no avail. He has a problem or two to solve at the cash register and in the kitchen and then returns to his station like a bishop. He knows no other way to deal with the night than to wrestle his way through it. Jazz is played at night; bars come alive then. Bradley's son, Jed, was asked in school what his father did. He said, "He sleeps all day and gets up and walks around in his pajamas."

We exchange anecdotes about Malcolm, who no longer works at the 55. He bought a house in Hoboken and now spends his time redoing it. He came into a small inheritance and no longer has to tend bar. He immediately developed high blood pressure. We discuss others who are gone, if not to Hoboken, forever. Tommy Flanagan plays this night in Bradley's. Every so often Bradley gets it into his head that it's been a long time between sets. Bradley has to worry about something now that he's not on the sauce. Flanagan, a scholarly-looking black man, moves in a leisurely fashion between tables. Not so long ago he played through the night with a heart attack and didn't know it until he got home. Bradley can't bring himself to rise and ask Flanagan to get back to the keyboard. Eventually Flanagan does and gentle but lively music fills the place. There are large, graphic portraits spotlighted on the wall and dark paneling. It's a settled, older crowd at the tables now, survivors of other raucous nights of the past. But ghosts abound.

At 4 A.M. there are fifty thousand people riding the subway in New York. That number is twice the size of my hometown when I was growing up. The other day my dentist was telling me: "My father-in-law has taken an interesting job. For him it's interesting. He likes it. He runs a token booth for the subway through the night. He was in business for himself up until he was sixty, in the dry-cleaning business, and he didn't have a pension. At sixty what're you going to do? He looked around and found this job that offered retirement benefits. He took an examination. . . . Now he goes to work around midnight and stays there until six. He's a shy man, it's perfect for him. He carries a transistor and plays it through the night. Maybe thirty or forty people come through wanting tokens. It's an out-of-the-way station, but he's not scared. He's in a bulletproof booth. He never goes out to collect tokens from the turnstiles unless a cop is there. . . . Here, rinse your mouth with this please. He drives to the station. . . . You know, he's always been a shy man and the kind that others always take advantage of. He'll wash the dishes and take out the trash, and if an errand needs to be done at home—like running out for aspirins or what have you—he's the one called upon. He loves that subway job and being away from people and alone at night. He's got his transistor to keep him company. He sleeps in the day. He doesn't see his wife as much. I've never seen him happier. OK, spit out, please."

The night force across the country is increasing, I learn. It rose by 5 percent from 1960 to 1976 for manufacturing workers in metropolitan areas. (The Bureau of Labor Statistics kept no figures on late-night workers before 1960.) For people moving into the dark hours to earn a living, it is a move into a vast unknown, sometimes happily, often in shock. No one has statistics on what it does to the body and mind. Only impressions exist and intuition. Night workers develop lousy sleep habits even if they're owls. They stay up for day pleasures—out to fish when the season opens, an afternoon at the races, getting the car fixed in the morning. They get sour stomachs, rampant piles, ulcers and constipation. They go home in the mornings dead-tired and then cannot sleep. Their diets aren't balanced. They take to the sauce, become chain smokers and depend on heavy doses of caffeine. *Fortune* magazine ran an article called "The Lonely World of Night Work" by David Morgolich, in which it was found that most night workers develop all the classic symptoms of chronic sleep deprivation, including fatigue and inefficiency. Drug addicts find their way to the night shift. Drugs are more easily gotten then and supervision is at a minimum. It's heaven for them. And the most stable marriages take a beating. During the night, lines form before the pay phones at plants, husbands checking up on spouses. ("Lucille, your voice sounds a little funny. Is there anyone there with you?" "You done woke me up. Course my voice sounds funny." "Just checking.")

Larry King's talk show is a solace for many. It goes out over the airways from Arlington, Virginia, every weeknight from midnight to 5:30 A.M. It is carried by more than two hundred stations of the Mutual Broadcasting System and is followed devotedly by around three million souls. The long-distance trucker dials him in, and the night watchman props himself back in a straight chair and nods in agreement when King scores a point. King, a forty-seven-year-old bespectacled man, fields questions and listens to opinions from those with gumption enough to dial his number. On nearly every radio at night there is some off-the-wall talk show to be found, with zany chatter and beyond-the-fringe commentary. This kind of talk one never finds by day. Callers' voices become slurred after 3 A.M., their contentions more baroque.

"Hello, Sam the Answer Man. I got a beef. I think all these girls running around in hot pants and see-through blouses should be put in stockades—like they did scarlet women back in Puritan days. It's a shame and disgrace and blight on civilization what some of these—" Patriotism comes to the fore. They want to nuke Iran, sink the entire land of Argentina and the British fleet, fly Old Glory from the top of every building. Listeners in those long-distance trucks, those holed up in rooming houses with insomnia, others relegated to being a night clerk in a tacky hotel talk back to the speaker. "You ignorant goddamn ninny! Who oughta be bombed is you, you son of a bitch!" Everyone seems to be drunk or drugged or crazy after a certain hour. A psychiatrist told me, "Anyone who is single and works nights at the post office is considered schizophrenic. No other facts need be known. It's automatic." Night is not sane like day. The full moon comes out.

And through it all, certain work gets done. Around midnight a computer shift changes on Wall Street. A moment before, the street is empty and quiet. Footsteps echo and a stray piece of paper whirls in the breeze, the picture of the usual deserted night scene. The Wall Street area can become very still with its narrow, winding streets that were built for a past century, the tall buildings towering and pressing from the sides. Bare as it is of a Sunday morning. Then—wham, bam—a mob scene with a horde of briefcase-laden figures pushing past the glass doors and crowding the street. An army of computer programmers. They duck down subway entrances, go for the parked cars, flag taxis. It's like any other after-work tableau except it's the middle of the night.

Wall Street is increasingly using the night to get its work done. When offices are redone—new flooring and paneling and arranging of space—it is done most often late at night. It won't interfere with day work. A contractor for this kind of work, a proficient ex-hippie, told me: "It's beautiful. No one around to bother you, no one to smear paint or knock over a power saw. You can tune in loud music. You can mellow out on grass, get stoned high as a kite and still get more done than you ever would by day. And they pay you extra to do it at night."

Japan offers cots for its industrial workers to take snoozes on during the night shift; a West German research institute screens those slated for night duty in that country, on the lookout for those who may be bad risks—people under twenty-five and over fifty, those with digestive problems, diabetics, epileptics, loners and the poor devils with noisy sleeping quarters. The AFL-CIO estimates that the number of people worldwide on the night shift has doubled in the last twenty years. Third World countries, trying for maximum use of available plants, keep machinery moving around the clock.

Things do not get rolling at Magique in New York until eleven at night. By 1 A.M. there are lines outside, people waiting to plunk down fifteen dollars to enter. Limousines are double-parked, yellow taxicabs easing in and out of a space in front, allowing legs in designer jeans to jut out and patrons alight. Drinks inside cost four dollars per and bars are set up at various strategic points. It is roomy, this disco. The deafening music plays nearly continuously, no tune discernibly different from the other, one song erupting into another. Couples boogaloo on the dance floor through hazy gray tobacco smoke, and now and then the word goes out that a celebrity has entered—B. J. Thomas, the singer, then Robert De Niro, the actor. (The wrong word goes out about De Niro. It is not him. It is a former numbers runner for a crime family, decked out in a plantation white suit, thin black tie, and a light blue wide-collar shirt. His black hair is slicked down and gleaming, patent leather style. He is basking in his De Niro look-alike status.)

No one seems to know what sort of people come to Magique. They are mostly youngish and fashionably got up and are hungry for something. For human contact? They all eyeball one another, as if trying to discover someone who really belonged in this pricey, eardrum-shattering milieu, the one regular. A row of mute, surly-looking young females lounge in a small space back of the dancing arena. They are a little too gaudily dressed, a little too made-up and quick with their eye contact. I ask a bartender what sort of people come to this place. He is twenty-ish, in a dark blue T-shirt, muscles bulging. Bartenders at discos must be hired as much for looks as for athletic ability in preparing drinks swiftly. "Oh, just people," he says. Drinks are cut off at four, but a hardcore of patrons hangs around until six, exiting into a bracing, windy dawn. I suspect a wide collection of people go there, making it in turn fashionable and sought after, because they believe more knowledgeable, more wealthy, more beautiful, more famous and wantonly sexual people than themselves go there. The discos are houses of mirrors.

Hospitals admit people twenty-four hours a day, often through the emergency room. Unfortunately it's impossible to know when one is due to enter or exit. My good friend Bert, a worldly man in the autumn of his years, was walking down the street not long ago when he ran into a filmmaker he knew. It was one of those busy, hectic, hand-shaking moments, two people in transit in the metropolis. Both are successful and high-powered and with a thousand things perking on the agenda. Their parting words were, "We've got to get together soon," the metropolis's standard words for people in a hurry. That evening, late, Bert collapsed from long-delayed nervous exhaustion and rapid, irregular heartbeat. As he lay on the cart in the hallway of the hospital, waiting for a room in which to be wheeled, he looked over and saw that the adjacent cart held none other than the filmmaker, tubes going into his arms and through his nose. Both managed a brief wince at each other in recognition, together sooner than expected.

A few summers ago I had no idea that I was destined for the emergency room either. I was diving into a cold mountain lake with my son Nick. It was just before the sun crossed the yard-arm, and I was thinking about a tall vodka and tonic to follow, perhaps more than one. Nick wore his orange Mark Spitz "swim-trainer" around his chest and he liked being thrown high in the air from a rock island into the deepest part of the water. I followed and we both came up, sputtering and happy. It was another one of those moments forever etched precisely in memory. "Let's do it one more time, Dad," I still hear. He was—and is—totally without physical fear. But he wanted me to carry him from the lake when we reached shallow water. I was doing so when I tripped over an underwater boulder and felt a sharp pain. Bright red blood was seeping from a gash on my lower shin when I reached shore, but I dismissed it. Who could get hurt in such a silly fashion? A vodka and tonic was on its way.

My brother-in-law Phil immediately applied a tight "butter-fly" bandage when we reached the cottage. He had received his medical training in the Boy Scouts. He suggested that I keep the bandage on for a week in order to avoid a scar. He did offer first, though, to drive me to a hospital's emergency room for a second opinion. It was up to me. But everything felt perfectly fine after a few vodka and tonics. Why cause a fuss? The next day the pain increased to a steady dull ache, but I could live with it. Another night passed. Finally, in the car with Lis and the kids, my leg elevated, I acknowledged that I might have something wrong. It could be a hairline fracture. I had once broken my leg skiing and the pain was not dissimilar. I admitted this possibility, and it was as if Lis had been waiting patiently to hear it ever since the accident. She drove immediately, no further words needed, to the hospital of a small town in the Catskills. It was a warm, sunny afternoon, but I felt chilled. I knew I would feel better when they X-rayed the leg and found no fracture. The mind can play tricks. The brisk, gray-haired nurse in the emergency room did not wait to take my name. She raised my purplish, swollen leg while we were both seated, placed it on her starched white lap and ripped off Dr. Phil's expert butterfly bandage. An ugly green froth oozed out of the gash. The gash had now raised a bump the size of a goose egg. She said, "We're admitting you to the hospital."

"But I only came to see if I had a fracture."

"You've got an infection."

"I'm going back home. I'll treat myself there."

"You don't want to die, do you?"

So began my two days and two nights in the Margaretville Hospital, my last view of the outside as I'm wheeled down a corridor reeking of antiseptic, the sight of Lis and the boys huddled together, their eyes big, her arms around each of their shoulders. The days passed in a noisy, sweaty jangle, filled with endless steps in the hallway outside my room, technicians and doctors and nurses syphoning blood from my body or asking me questions. It was rational and busy and a pain. The nights were cooler and quieter and filled with mystery (hallucinations?).

I lay flat out on my bed, my left arm strapped down and receiving pints of high-voltage penicillin that entered a vein there via a long needle. (The vein had been elusive and hard to hit.) I never slept, as far as I know. Nurses whisked in to change the penicillin bottles, efficient and as impersonal as airline stewardesses. I smelled each one as she reached to change the penicillin bottle and take away my deposit of pee I'd left in a contraption you could plug yourself into while horizontal. I smelled their sweetish perfume and recently soaped faces and their lipstick. I listened to their rubber soles squeak and their starched white uniforms crinkle as they moved. Sometimes their hose made a whisper, too, as they strode.

Suddenly, in the wee hours, a man in a not overly clean white jacket bent over me. His black hair was sparse and he had a stubble of beard. His belly pooched out the white hospital jacket. "How you doing, Mac?" He rather tenderly drew back my bed covers and, after donning surgical gloves, inspected my leg. I could see a small red streak coming up the side of my leg toward my groin. It had about six inches to go. I really didn't want to see that. I remembered that a President's son had died in the White House from blood poisoning, something that had started from a blister he'd got on his heel while playing tennis.

"How does it look?" I asked the man. I didn't know who he was.

"Looks like you got yourself a humdinger there." He wrapped it in a hot towel and then put a heating pad around that. "Is that too hot for you? Don't want to get her too hot and make you uncomfortable."

"No, that's fine. I didn't think this was anything at the time. You know, just a bump when I fell over a big stone in a lake. Seems silly."

"I've seen 'em start from just a tiny scratch. Nothing at all. Then it swells and starts moving toward a vital organ. Once it gets in a vital organ it goes right to your brain and that's it."

"What do you think my chances are? From what you see here. Do you think it's going to be all right?"

"I'm no doctor."

He was a nurse. He drew a chair up beside my bed and took a break. He was an ex-fireman from New York, a man who had put in his twenty years and retired. From there he had taken nurse's training at Hunter College. The Fire Department encouraged early retirement for those who went into nurse's training. There was a nursing shortage; there was a long list of applicants wanting to be firemen. "I saw enough burning buildings down in the city," he told me. "I saw everything—'roasts,' what we called burned corpses, fires that lasted for days. I was a harbor fireman. I put out wharfs and docks and ships that caught on fire. Nursing is a breeze."

He came to the Catskills because he liked the hunting and fishing in the area. He owned a mobile trailer in Phoenicia which he docked beside the Esopus Creek. Since he had little seniority on the nursing staff, he was placed on the night shift at the hospital. He was a bachelor. He drew his chair up closer. "They got a lot of feisty broads down in Phoenicia. You ever go to any of the bars there?" This was my nurse talking.

"I've put in my time in them. But I'm married now. I hardly ever go in one now."

"Listen"—closer to the bed, male camaraderie, possibly not wanting me to think, perish the thought, he might be effeminate since he was a nurse—"they've got broads I never seen anything like right there in Phoenicia. You know Roxanne—big broad, head of blond hair, jokes a mile a minute, drink you under the table? Hey, boobs way out to here?"

"Sounds like somebody I might know."

"Don't tell anyone, but we're a duo. The reason I don't want you to tell anyone is that she's married. You wouldn't believe what goes on in Phoenicia. If I told you, you wouldn't believe it. You've heard of Peyton Place. Phoenicia is Peyton Place."

I saw from the black plastic tag with thin white lettering that my nurse's name was Ralph. We were not unlike two guys sitting around a bar, batting the breeze, except I lay prone in bed, penicillin dripping into my vein and Ralph wore a short white jacket, a stethoscope dangling from a side pocket. He told me that he got to hunt and fish during the season to his heart's content, because he didn't work days. "That's what I like about working nights. You're free to enjoy nature in the daytime. Why live up here if you can't enjoy nature. And this is the greatest spot of land anywhere on earth. You could travel the whole world and never find anything as green, the water as pure, the hunting and fishing so good. I don't know how I ever lived in the city."

Ralph comes throughout the night to change the wet bandage on my leg. Swathes of time pass and suddenly he's there, wiggling his surgical gloves on. I can see at a sharp angle out a casement window a sliver of the mountain outside. I prize the meager view. It's all I have of the outside. I hear the wind rustling the trees and see by moonlight the tall pines sway. A brief mountain storm passes. A fog settles in the ridge of the mountain and, as dawn breaks, is burned away in the hot red streaks of the sun. A very old woman in white comes now to whisk away my jug of pee. "Have you ever been to Germany?" she says abruptly.

"Yes, I have."

"I went for the first time last year." She rests a hand against the bedside table; the other holds the pee. "We took the Icelandic airline and landed in Luxembourg. We then took a train . . ." She gives me a detailed account of her trip, each stop, each meal, each person encountered. The highlight was attendance of the Passion play at Oberammergau. "I'd yearned all my life to see that play. It's marvelous, magnificent, just beyond anything I had imagined." The poor woman doesn't have many teeth. She puts the jug back on the nightstand, because it's becoming too heavy in her hand. She relates every scene in the Passion play, tells me about each character and critiques each performance. She tells me the history of the Passion play, its ups and downs. I cannot leave; I look at the ceiling and the new fresh light of day. I could ring for the nurse with my right hand, but this is the nurse. She asks me if I believe in Christ—and I say I guess I do—and she leaves.

The corpulent cleaning woman arrives cheerily, mop handle flying around my bed. She has worked through the night. The heat shield is off my wound for the moment and she views the wound reflectively with a frown. I ask her what she thinks. "I'm no doctor. I don't want to get into no diagnosing." The day warms up feverishly and then cools off into twilight. When long shadows appear, my doctor is sitting in a chair near the open casement window. He may have been talking for a while before I notice him. He is a "dropout," one of many who have discovered the Catskills. There are ex-Wall Street brokers hammering nails here; former models herding goats; once-upon-a-time rug salesmen running Yoga meditation centers. By all rights my doctor should be practicing medicine in New York City. He grew up and went to private schools there. His medical training pointed him that way. Instead, he is a country doctor. He is outfitted by L. L. Bean, right down to his boots and socks. He wears a lumberjack's flannel shirt unbuttoned at the neck and khaki pants. New York City doctors are like the day—regular, going along to the same drummer; my doctor is the night. He is telling me why he has chosen this wild, hard-bitten area of the Catskills to live in.

"The chlorophyll percentage is high here. I firmly believe that the days of this earth are numbered. Oh, yes . . . I'm serious." I'm thinking about my wound and wondering what the latest diagnosis is. "You can pick out spots that have an intensity of greenness and then count how many people are there. You can do it on a slide rule. The greener the location and the fewer the people, the higher the survival level. People on a desert will be finished in no time. Those in cities like New York will die off immediately. Places like Margaretville will hold the key to life continuing itself." He holds his chin in his hand.

Margaretville. It had a restaurant/bar called Mother's on its main drag which was recently boarded over. It had looked attractive and I had meant to visit it, but, like so many enterprises in the town, it had sunk, gone under. (Nelson Algren has written, "Never eat at a place called Mom's, never play poker with a man called Doc, and never go to bed with a woman who has more troubles than your own.") But there was a primeval cast to the region. Many times I had walked in forests that bore no trace of humankind; the lush greenness fairly dripped. A chorus came from the birds and animals and insects and there seemed to be a muted sound even from the growing plants. It burst with life in spring. My doctor seemed to read my thoughts: "You know, I drive along some back road late at night here and I get the eerie feeling that I'm lost in time. It could be the beginning of life. . . . The way the fog settles and rises, the absolute stillness, the silent, full silver moon. The hush. It's enduring here. Those smart enough and lucky enough to end up here will survive."

I'm thinking about dying here. Now, in deep night, a total blackness out the casement window, no footfalls outside, I visualize what it might be like to die. A spirit could easily take its leave in this room—no sun giving warmth, no signs of life around. You could just breathe deeply (a death rattle?) and let go. . . . So long, everybody. A giant curtain would fall, and all concerns would cease. I wouldn't have to think about work or growing old or my tennis game slipping. I wouldn't have to worry about death then.

I wondered if my obituary would make the *Times*. At best a short, three-column deal with no picture. Lis got things done and that was something she'd see to. Maybe I'd be described as a novelist-journalist "whose first book, etc." . . . I could picture the gang at the 55 getting the news. Many wouldn't remember me—or anything. Some people from Tennessee might. My boys would only have a dim memory—a funny old guy who liked to lift them on his shoulders. . . . The drops fall silently from the overhead bottle into the tube leading to my vein. I fret each time the bottle nears Empty and no nurse is in sight—I feel that if that penicillin stops I will say *adios* to it all.

A color TV is perched on the wall at the foot of my bed. With my free hand I operate a remote-control gadget that allows me to select the channel and loudness of sound I want. I love it, adore it. The set at home has a bent coat hanger for an antenna. A quarter of the screen, at the bottom, has developed a mysterious black bar across it, squeezing the lower part of the picture up. Thus the Miss America Contest in September appears with smiling, normal-headed young bathing beauties with the tiniest of legs. Now I wallow in an all-night sea of colored normal-sized junk. Merv Griffin has aged and become slicker since last I saw him; ditto, Johnny Carson. They are elderly by all rights and beloved by their audiences. I don't know any of the "guests," but they all look the same—men with open-necked shirts and medallions dangling and smiling, slender, white-teethed women with plenty of newly washed hair. I relish flicking the stations around, omnipotent in a hospital wing with no other sound—like on the moon. "Blow it out your barracks bag," I can —and do—sling back at whoever is on deck. The night passes. I watch a whole Clark Gable movie. Films were simpler then— good and evil defined. Gable got the girl; he also displayed a wide banjo seat in tight khakis.

My nurse strolls in to take my temperature and blood pressure and change my hot, wet pad, a fresh whiff of tobacco and malt on his breath. "How can you watch that shit?" he says. "I never look at it anymore. I'd rather go fishing or chase broads. I'm going to get me some down in Phoenicia tomorrow night. Is that too hot for you?" Another nurse arrives on creaky rubber soles and swiftly gives me a penicillin refill. Stations drop off the air with the national anthem playing and shots of jets roaring through the sky. Stations pop to life at dawn with announcers chomping at the bit to present the news. Life and problems to be solved again! Footfalls sound in the hall. . . . A team of doctors poke at my wound. It doesn't hurt; the puffy redness has gone down and the dreaded crimson death streak is fading. "You can get out today."

As I hobble toward the front entrance, dressed in civvies and ready to heave myself back again into the family VW, I hear a loud, cheery bellow behind me. "Wait, wait!" It is my doctor. He's in his lumberjack shirt and khakis. "We gave you the wrong penicillin!"

"The wrong penicillin?"

"We just got the results on the culture back from the lab. It was a different kind of bug than we thought got you. Here, take this ampicillin when you get home."

"You mean all those bottles that went into me was of no use. All that stuff in my veins . . . ?"

"Listen, man, you made it. Medicine is partly an occult science anyhow. You're alive. That's what counts. Let's have a beer together sometime."

Ten

BEYOND THE ARCTIC CIRCLE whole populations become "night" people whether they want to or not. To live there is to live by night for a good part of the year. In Tromsø, Norway (pop. 45,850), the people do not see the sun from November 25 until January 21. Norwegians name this dark period *mørketiden* —"the murky time." Edwin Kiester, Jr., a science writer, did a study of this town for *Geo* magazine. He found that people got crankier then than during the midnight suns of July. They slept more fitfully. Crime increased and families split up more frequently. It was particularly hard for men over fifty who lived alone. Many took to the bottle or went crazy or both. Explorers of the polar region from Amundsen to Byrd have recorded experiencing bizarre hallucinations as they began being deprived of light and engulfed by night. *Mørketiden* makes for fierce competitors, too. A study of winter-sports achievements of athletes from the dark parts of Scandinavia showed far more of them in the winner's circle than those from southern regions.

Outwardly Tromsø seems a bustling 1980s city. Kiester found "supermarkets, cinemas, a 10,000-student university, fish canneries, insurance offices, even a Burger King." People worked harder in the dark time of year, students attended more lectures; there were more social and family gatherings, and people huddled together more than in summer.

The pineal gland secrets its hormone, melatonin, in darkness and supresses it in natural and artificial light. In animals a decrease in melatonin increases fertility—thus, more light, more offspring. Many farmers keep lights on in the hen house and they get many more eggs. They trick a hen's endocrine system into thinking it's spring. In Tromsø the dark winter nights are softened by the flame of electricity. Kiester ran across houses with as many as twelve lighted windows, in addition to flood-lighted driveways and gardens. A Tromsø family uses three times as much power as an average American family. And Tromsø society indulges in many rituals to get them through the endless nights. Restaurants are filled, and the townspeople spend more money on restaurant meals than do residents of any other Norwegian city.

People throw parties and have family gatherings. They try their best not to be alone. To be alone and in the dark is to be vulnerable and risk going bananas. In Tromsø they celebrate Christmas nearly the entire *mørketiden.* The festivities begin around December 10 and last until mid-January. There is an arch of light down the entire main street to remind people of the missing sun. They eat a lot; figures balloon. The first day that the sun appears during the new year is a time for celebration. It is a holiday, called Sol Day (Sun Day). There is a town parade, complete with a Sun Princess. The sun rises at 11:56 and sets at noon—a four-minute day—but with a sliver of light from above, nothing man-made, there is a reminder of the earth's orbit and the endless days of summer to follow.

And with daylight, children in Tromsø may cease fearing the trolls, those evil, funny-looking little people who live in the darkest part of the forest and who are turned to stone by daylight.

Ted Klein is editor in chief of *Twilight Zone,* a magazine of the supernatural and the horrific. Ted is trim and casually turned out and his eyes peer intently through substantial lenses. He does not sleep at night as a regular thing. Having to energet-ically charge into an office in the morning makes him reluc-tantly turn in early—say, at three-thirty. Otherwise he would greet the dawn and feel all's right with the world once more. There is something comforting in watching a new day begin, seeing the new light shining, hearing a dog's morning bark, feeling the pulse of life gaining momentum once more, smell-ing the new day. It's safety and security for Ted. He stays up to greet the day, and he admits that he is afraid of the dark. He stays up through it because he fears it. He doesn't want to sink into it through sleep. His childhood fear of the dark has never diminished. "Maybe it's why I'm into horror stories," he says.

Joe, a South Carolinian in New York, finds himself getting jumpy around nine at night. For a while he couldn't figure out why. At eight he might be dining or stepping into a movie or pouring a drink. All would be running along smoothly—and then at nine, out of the blue, comes an acute edginess. His eye turns to the clock. It finally came to him that he was jumpy because back in South Carolina they closed the joints and rolled up the sidewalks at nine. To be an owl in a small Southern town is to be sentenced to purgatory. The larks run everything. A stillness spreads over the land at nine, and the decree is to start preparing for bed. What does an owl do? He moves to New York.

There are couples caught in an owl/lark dilemma. At first mating they didn't realize the breach in their sleep habits, but time tells. A man's internal clock may ring at six in the morning. He rolls out, jogs a mile or two, fixes breakfast while listening to the news. He is in his office by eight, before anyone else. All the while his wife lies comatose in bed, blankets pulled over her head, dead to the world. Left to her own devices, she might sleep till three. Her motor doesn't start revving until at least six that night. And she stays up until four—long after her husband has conked out midway through the eleven o'clock news.

I once worked in an office where I could overhear (unfortunately) conversations from another unit. Every day, late in the afternoon, a dynamo of an executive would call home. Earlier through the day I had listened to him harangue and goad employees under him. Now, at close of day, as summer light dimmed on the skyscraper opposite or, in winter, a Black Hole presented itself outside, the man would croon, "Oh—hello, darling. Did I wake you?" Was this wife being a prima donna? Was she outfitted in a tight pink gown like Mae West, snoozing and perhaps boozing between nibbles of bonbons? I couldn't figure her—or the situation—out. "Hello, darling. Did I wake you?"

Now I believe I know the answer: He had hitched up to an owl. I picture a nighttime scene of the dynamo running down, his chin sinking to his chest, his toupee slipping off, his words slurring. Before him his wife—a short, stocky blonde—hitting her stride. She is discussing the winter Miami vacation, a son's school marks, a Broadway play—all simultaneously. She is really getting going. She treads on through the night, reading a bit, catching TV, alone. Some people are born to appreciate and flourish in the dark time. Couples work out their own rhythms. Sometimes it may be a blessing not to see that much of each other. Some couples indeed make it to golden wedding anniversaries on lark/owl schedules. They make dates for sex, if one can believe feature articles and TV broadcasts on the subject. One of them suffers the pangs of hell just by rising and having breakfast with his mate; the other may herself nod off while indulging her husband's whim for a late-night supper.

Dr. Elliot D. Weitzman, the late director of the sleep-wake disorders center at Montefiore Hospital in the Bronx, felt that a natural rhythm of sleep patterns may well be set by genetics. We have it at birth. The truly extreme—those whose natural inclination is to stay awake through the entire night, or to rise at dawn and skip through the day, collapsing at dark—compose about 5 to 10 percent of the population. They can do nothing about it. Human sleep averages between seven and eight hours a clip, but the range of normal sleep is between four and ten hours. Some healthy people sleep but one to three hours a night. It's not insomnia for them, but how they're made—as some of us are tall, some short. Albert Einstein slept almost half the day, but Thomas Edison often had to be driven to bed, existing on four hours of sleep at night with a few naps during the day. Short sleepers are deep sleepers, and move quickly into stage-four sleep on the rapid-eye-movement (REM) dream sleep. Dr. Ernest Hartman, head of the sleep laboratory at Boston State Hospital, has found that short sleepers are usually highly efficient and energetic, can-do people, who don't brood over matters but push problems aside. He's found that long sleepers are more "tortured" and use the dreams of a long night to alleviate emotional problems.

Some find a natural rhythm in indulging their weaknesses and secret sins late at night. George, a college friend of mine, reads through the night—accompanied by a jug of cognac. He goes through Dickens, Balzac, Wells, revelations on the CIA, and German textbooks, sipping Rémy Martin and letting the stillness and night air settle over him. That is his *natural* bent; at times he has to take a job and his instinct is curbed.

More than one fat person has told me about the solace of the refrigerator late at night. Its steady hum comforts them. In a darkened kitchen its pop-on light sends a shiver of pleasure down the spine. You can gorge at night and no one is the wiser. It puts more pounds on you, but what the hell. I see a woman in a loose tent-sized garment bent over at the fridge, a warm, pale light spreading from the fridge. Her behind, the size of a bass drum, is raised to the heavens. She is after that turkey leg, that roll of liverwurst, the pimiento loaf, the wedge of chocolate cake. Up in the freezing compartment lies a mound of brick ice cream. On the radio, waiting, is the late night wisdom of Larry King. No one can find her. No one can tell her no. Heaven.

Those who received genes marked "ordinary, no extremes" find it maddening to be placed on the night shift. Jobs require it though—and more and more so. Statistically one out of every five employed person in this country works at night. It affects the white-collar worker now as well as the blue-collar. In New York seven hundred people in white collars are still working for Chase Manhattan as the sun sets. All over there are little pockets here and there and certainly not in what we've always thought of as nighttime professions. They are not enjoying the late-night food binge. They aren't reading Dickens or being alone with their thoughts. They are doing what others do in the day, only at night. They come at you half crazy: "I despise my life, this working nights, but I got to do it. It's wrecking the hell out of my social life. Social life! I haven't got one. My sex life is zero. My body seems to sleepwalk through the hours. I'm there and I'm not there. It's killing me."

Doctors say that nighttime workers (as opposed to day) develop more gastrointestinal disorders. They are prone to hardening of the arteries. Night work can be a killer to some. The night worker does not eat properly, has trouble getting the right sleep in the day. A mother who works nights tells me, "I find I'm screaming at my kids a lot more during the day. I'm run down. My nerves are on edge." A young man tells me that he has lost his friends by working nights. He's become a loner. Night work is a frontier and hard for most to come naturally to terms with. The joys of watching the sun rise, driving on nonrush-hour highways and having days free for a baseball game pale beside the physical and mental price it costs many.

Mary Ellen works in a massage parlor where she goes by the name Candy. She is plump and has pale, bad skin which she camouflages with a couple of layers of makeup. She could be twenty-five or thirty or forty, but after talking with her a while one realizes she's indeed a young teenager—despite the casual extensive knowledge she holds of glorified whoredom and the experiences thereof, despite an initial toughness and wariness. She came from a small town in New England to Manhattan and soon met a man named Perez who immediately (the same night) became her vocational counselor. Her tales about him make him sound cruel and conniving, but she professes love. *"He* locked me in a room all last week because he suspected I'd made contact with another fellow, a friend of his. I hadn't, I swear I hadn't, never in a million years would I have done that. But Perez got mad and jealous and locked me up. He gave me some Ritz crackers and Coke and I had to live on that. He beat me when he let me out. But now we're fine. I'm bringing in a lot of bucks and he's looking after me."

This means that Perez cares for her. Anyone willing to beat her and mistreat her, anyone taking the time and effort, getting involved, must care. It is not unlike the posture of her father. She tells me that she comes from a large family in Massachusetts, an Irish Catholic family, where the father ruled with an iron hand. He beat her over being out late on dates, about poor grades, over certain attitudes she assumed.

Mary Ellen thought the bright lights of Manhattan would solve her problems. She would be somebody and not be forced to live under the strictures of a solemn, no-nonsense dad. She then fit right in with the beatings and discipline administered by Perez. She is but one of many women in his stable, as she was but one of many sisters whipped and shamed by a father. Perez has put her on the street, in hotel lobbies and now in a massage parlor to ply her trade. She says she is happy. To her this is glamorous, the idea of being an *outlaw,* surviving in the Big Apple, someone who is paid attention to. She works, as we say, nights.

"Most of the high-rolling johns come in after two in the morning. You know, they get soused in a bar or a girl friend won't put out, and they get horny and don't want to go home. Married guys, too. Lots of married guys. They drift in. I don't see them as people. They're just bodies and faces and smells. Listen, guys can stink. Their feet, their lousy bodies. They think I don't matter, that's what kills me. They think, Here's a hooker, I don't have to be anything but my lovable self. What does it matter with her? I lie. I tell them they're wonderful, they're just terrific. I fake an orgasm. I steal from them. Little do they know."

Night passes with a series of bodies; occasionally with a police bust. The place has a linoleum rug, worn brown in spots, curtained cubicles and an abiding scent of Lysol. The light is low wattage. She works in tight hot pants, stiletto heels and a tight jersey blouse. She removes articles of clothing on viewing the size of the customer's bankroll and by the apparent extent and ease with which he imparts his whoredom knowledge. If he says he wants a "local," she knows that here is a man who has had fellatio in a rub joint before. It gets pretty degrading. Copulation is consummated on the slightly damp massage table. Shortly before dawn, after the last john has weaved in from a bar and found himself impotent, Mary Ellen is picked up by Perez. Either picked up personally or she meets him in an all-night diner or an after-hours bar. He can be capricious on timing. He looks good after the lineup of johns. He smells of a pervasive cologne and his mod boots shine. His wide-brimmed felt hat is all style. He is funny at dawn, she tells me, and often high on cocaine. Pimps and their women snort cocaine and take Quaaludes; johns drink booze. They occupy different stations. Hookers think theirs is better.

I talked to Mary Ellen on a late afternoon (or early evening) at her dentist's. (So often is a dentist the go-between for something or other; it may be in compensation for never quite becoming a doctor. Dentists are strivers for something more. They appreciate art and start talent agencies and run for political office. They are not night people, but a bundle of energy for the day.) Her dentist is a charming, soft-spoken man in glasses and fine tailoring. He smiles contentedly. A hooker is in his reclining chair, having her teeth done. Another waits in the outer salon while Mary Ellen chats with me in his small private office. The good dentist simply likes hookers. The word spreads through the underground and he is kept busy with their dental complaints. They pay in cash because they never have checking accounts. They don't show up in early morning. Twilight is when they are just getting moving.

A male friend of the dentist's, a dilettante of the outlaw nether world, is in an unused patient's room, sunk back in a reclining chair, taking whiffs of nitrous oxide (laughing gas) through a rubber face mask. It gives him a high. In the waiting room eyes are shaded by dark glasses. The dentist is as happy as a clam. A fly in the ointment is the fear that a disgruntled pimp may bust in with trouble on his mind, looking for one of his women and carrying a piece. An aspect of the hooker's world (and the nether night region) is that violence buzzes around it and often stings. I remember one victim, a plump, sultry-looking woman with slight bags under her eyes. She had talked with me and told me of narrow escapes from johns who went berserk. Her specialty was bondage. One of her protectors in the field had once barged into the dentist's office while she lay supine and undergoing a drilling and had shouted threats in her ear. She took the trouble to have her hair cut stylishly and her teeth checked regularly and she was very much alive. Then suddenly she made the *Daily News*. Her battered and stabbed body was found in her Upper East Side apartment; an alert was out for her missing boyfriend, wanted for questioning.

The threat of a violent end seeps into their consciousness as it does into fighter pilots'. They joke and relish yarns about it. Fools, to them, are the yo-yos who work nine to five, who take the ordinary daylight path. Night holds spectacular terrors and vast joys unknown to the dull daytime marchers. Hookers comport themselves as superior. It angers them if anyone dares to pity them.

A while back in Las Vegas I met Joanie. She worked nights although, in the heart of the casinos, there is no day or night. Things go full tilt here twenty-four hours a day. That first eve-

ning we talked she wore all white—shoes and purse, everything. She had the blond good looks of a healthy and efficient
secretary in a small Southern bank. She reeked of primness and
a spinster's wariness. We sat facing one another at a table in one
of the multitude of cocktail lounges at Caesar's Palace. Her face,
at nine o'clock in the evening, showed slight puffiness from
recent sleep. Her day was just beginning. She told me that her
father, now deceased, had been a fairly well-known politician in
Mississippi. Her mother had since remarried a younger man
and had become something of a hedonist. Joanie herself had
never fit in with small-town Mississippi society. She had always
dreamed of somewhere else to go, someplace more romantic.
While working in an office in her hometown, she had had an
affair with a friend's husband. That was as daring as she had
been. She had come on what she considered a brief vacation to
Vegas, passing through, and had lazily let time and her money
run out. A woman she met from a nearby apartment convinced
her that turning a trick was an easy way to earn a buck. Joanie
went to one of the clubs on the Strip in an evening gown, got
picked up for the night and made enough to bail herself out of
debt. She became a working girl.

Television had already prepared the way. "I used to watch
Miss Kitty on 'Gunsmoke' and envy her. She was who I wanted
to be. Don't tell me she wasn't a working girl either. How'd she
get her money? Why was she hanging out in a saloon? She was
turning tricks, that's why, and she took no shit. I don't like to
take shit. Never have. And I've always run with people who got
a lot out of life. Even in high school, when I still had my cherry, I
hung out with girls who had hot pants, those who gave out a
little piece now and then. . . ."

Joanie had "juice" at several clubs along the Strip. She was
permitted by security guards to sit on divans in the lobby and
occupy space in the bars, and they turned their heads when she
left for a room with a hotel guest. A trick might take Joanie
forty-five minutes, and then she was back on the divan or sipping club soda in the bar. The one-armed bandits crank away
through the night in Vegas, the dice rattle, ice clinks and a
steady buzzing sound passes through the crowded casinos. It's a
childhood fantasy to be stranded there—all things for pleasure,

everyone allowed to stay up forever. There is also the cutting edge of danger to make the senses stay alive and awake.

Around five in the morning, no johns in sight, Joanie went for a big meal in the hotel's fluorescently lit coffee shop. She behaved as if still on a schoolgirl's budget, deciding on a hamburger deluxe because of the extras attached. Away from the divan and barstool she became the prim office worker taking her working meal. She knew busboys and some of the waitresses. She took on a somewhat cocky stance, as if she were living the glamorous, dangerous gunslinger's role and the waitresses were ordinary troops. She was the one who went out on hair-raising missions while the waitresses played it safe. But there was a bravado that went a little too far. She ate hastily and didn't linger over coffee, not because she didn't have the time and deserved a rest break, but because these ordinary workers made her uneasy after a while. She went from strutting like a duchess to reacting like a pariah. Historical courtesans may be lauded; plain old whores are scorned.

At daybreak she took me in her small, jazzy sports car to visit her apartment, which was well away from the casinos. She had made five hundred dollars for that evening's work. She told me on the drive over about an affair she was just ending with a man in the same housing complex. He had a mother fixation, she explained, wanting Joanie to read his mother's letters aloud right before lovemaking. He kept a diary in which he recounted every memory he could bring back about his mother. Joanie had to assume his mother's name before his passion was triggered. She told me this as some other person might have mentioned a suitor's table manners or the school he had gone to.

Her apartment was on well-kept grounds, a swimming pool and tennis court adjacent. Her apartment itself was neatly kept, with nothing out of the ordinary—no whips hanging from the walls or red lights glowing. There were framed family pictures, a color TV set in a prominent spot, expensive modern furniture, no mess at all in the kitchen, the air conditioners humming. There were a few messages from her answering service, which she took with nods of her head, expression stoical, and then she brought out a journal she had been keeping for many years. She read me passages in which she sung the praises of her best friend's husband back in Mississippi, in words lyrical and at the same time modest. There were descriptions of Nevada scenery and her feelings at various moments. Nothing in the journal was salacious. Nothing was there that hinted that through the nights she jumped in and out of the sack with whoever could rustle up fifty or a hundred dollars.

She brought out the family picture album. There was no mistaking that the Technicolored scenes were in the South—a bevy of bright flowers, grape arbors, the deep green grass. Her mother was a plumper, blonder version of herself in the photos, her sisters a little plainer than Joanie. It was a setting of affluence and comfort and many smiles. It was somewhere else. The sun was brightly shining in all the pictures.

I left the apartment at first light, a gentle, dry grayness seeping across the Vegas landscape. I left Joanie still flipping through her album, her feet curled up under her on the sofa. She was free until ten o'clock the coming night.

Eleven

SUDDENLY AWAKE. The creaky noise sounds from someplace outside the window—a whiny screech that is heard nowhere else on earth. I have spent hours in the middle of the night trying to pinpoint what it is—a whirring, groaning scrape of metal—that inexplicably rips the air at odd moments. I have discussed it with Lis. It comes windward from Geldzahler's digs. We have eliminated sources. It is not an air conditioner. It comes in dead of winter as well as summer. It is not a flagpole, although don't rule it out. Who would fly the flag in these parts? What-oh-what is it? Schemes bloom in the night as one lies flat-out in bed. I see myself asking Geldzahler if it is all right to investigate his roof to see if we can find out what it is, to explain that a whirring noise somewhere in his vicinity is driving us bats. I see him bemusedly permitting this excursion and understanding our need. GGGGGGrrrrrrrr. . . .

Yells and screams now from above—a male and female, the female weeping. "I'm only happy two hours a day with you! Only two hours a day am I happy!"

"Christ! Goddamnit!" A screech from the man, obliterating the metal screech from Geldzahler's place. Sometimes they rehearse a play above, the woman a budding actress. But this has an emotional depth, a heartfeltness beyond her competence as an actress. I wouldn't have expected the man to screech out of control. On the elevator, in public view, they seem happy and content together. What did she mean—only happy two hours a day? That statement edges its way into my dreamy state. I see twenty-four hours laid out as a gigantic pie and a wedge of two hours being scooped out. Lis doesn't let me know she's awake, too, but later she tells me that the woman's wail about being happy for just two hours each day intrigues her also. Poor little hapless woman, weeping for twenty-two hours then sunny and bright and happy for two. At what?

Creak . . . creak . . . creak. . . . I count my bills. But now facing the ongoing ticker tape of sums is a new image, an ally: Smilin' Jack, the Publisher. What a handsome, boyish face! How engaging! This handsome driving Force now stands in front of the advancing Black Glob. My book will be published! My characters will have a home. It'll not be just me who has gone to bed and awakened with them for so long—but soon they will move out to visit a teacher in Des Moines, a farmer in Virginia, an actor or somebody in Chicago. Others! It'll be between covers. Hell, they can check it out of the library if they're broke. I've watched my other books age like me in the Jefferson and Donnell libraries. Sentences have been underlined, pages ripped out (in anger or to carry home?). Between covers! Those typed sheets with chicken stratches all over them turned into dignified print between covers. Smilin' Jack called me on the phone. Let's hear his words, or an approximation, once more: "Your book reminds me of Nathanael West. It's in that category. I like it a lot. Let's meet for a drink."

Playback, once more, the Drink. It's after work, a late winter's day in Manhattan, a cold, chilling rain falling. It is dark when I leave the apartment. I wear the usual: Paul Stuart spring suit, Brooks shirt and tie, and the Brazilian loafers from Bloomies. The hole in the paper-thin soles of the loafers make walking not dissimilar to going barefoot. But outwardly the shoes look sharp and with-it, far preferable to donning L. L. Bean brogans. Over my head I carry a Korean umbrella purchased on an emergency basis from a Fourteenth Street vendor, who offered me a job.

We are to meet at a fancy-sounding French bistro on Thirty-fourth Street. I take the subway, then walk to the address. I'm a little early—don't want to seem pushy—so circle the block a couple of times. I can feel my socks getting soaked through the Brazilian slippers. At the bistro I find the door locked but lights on inside. I knock. The cold rain is really coming down, near icicles. There is a mistake. Smilin' Jack wouldn't torment me. A French lady in a smock pads out to the door. I see cozily lit tables inside, a bar with an array of multicolored bottles, smell hot bread and freshly cut flowers. Smilin' Jack has good taste. "The restaurant doesn't open till seven."

"But I'm to meet someone here at six."

"No, we don't open till seven. Would you like to make a reservation?"

"No, thanks."

The door shuts. Now what? I can try to call his office. But won't it be closed? Did I get the wrong restaurant? How could I possibly invent the name of this one though? Wrong time? Seven o'clock wouldn't be the hour for an after-work drink. I definitely heard six as the hour. I could get mad and leave in a huff—but what would that solve? It would sink the chances of his taking my book forever and then what? No, wait. Just wait patiently as you have up till now about everything on God's green earth. Stand out here in the fucking rain and early dark and wait for an answer. Not many people are passing. It bustles around here during the day but closes shop at night. I see various dark, lone forms loom on the horizon at Park and then descend toward me. Once or twice I'm sure it's Smilin' Jack, but the form materializes into an ordinary office laborer, someone with shoulders slumped, face pale, step heavy, a sad sack. A drop of rain runs over my nose and down my chin. Would Philip Roth and John Updike be out here cooling their heels? Bruce Jay makes deals and unwinds at Elaine's; they put Mario up in a suite at the Beverly Hills, limo him around and pay him a million dollars to turn out a hundred-page screenplay. Are we in the same profession? Am I in a profession?

Things blur in New York, particularly at night. Impressions come fleetingly, starkly, and then fade into the next—the madwoman in tatters, the taxi careening, a backfire on the order of a cannon, the halo of a lit skyscraper glimpsed through a foggy mist. Here comes some silly fuck in a babushka. It's Jack with a scarf tied around his head to ward off the raindrops. He's an aristocrat, set to do whatever is necessary and not asking anyone's permission. It's raining and no umbrella? Put the nearest thing over your head—a catcher's mitt, the New York *Times*, whatever. Get the job done. Never apologize, never explain. The restaurant doesn't open till seven? Forget it—we'll step across the street. Jack moves at a fast clip, wham bang, making decisions. Decisions are tossed left and right like the pope's blessings. One place looks a little morose, try the next, Jack in the lead. It's another Frenchie joint with a small, intimate bar in back. Jack decides yes, and checks his scarf and briefcase (actually a shopping bag crammed with books and manuscripts). I trail along (trailing water like a wet sheep dog), still waiting for I know not what. Jack continues at office tempo, a lark in the growing dark. I feel I am waking up.

We take barstools and face one another. We talk college, the Marine Corps, mutual friends, great ladies of our past, child rearing, the rent squeeze in Manhattan, literature and sheer shit. I am an owl, blinking my eyes in the deepening night. Suddenly I blurt out, "Jack, I'd really like for my book to end up at your house." He looks at me with a possum smile. He takes a finger load of peanuts to his mouth. He gets a cigarette off the barmaid, because he has cut down on smoking and is not buying. He nods. We part at the subway.

A week or so later he calls. His secretary comes on first, asks if I am me. I'm on "hold" for a while. Then Jack comes on in a rush. He's assigning my book to one of the bright young editors under him. I learn that it is a woman in her twenties, someone in high school when my first book came out. She has a glowing reputation. I tell Lis and the boys and our little family breaks out the champagne—a bottle we've been hoarding for a year. The boys can't quite grasp what we're celebrating, but they throw themselves into it. They throw themselves between our arms. Nick does cartwheels. David leaps off the sofa onto his head.

I lie in bed now and let the memory of the Drink and the Call lap back and forth over my mind like the tide. Creeeeeech . . . from Geldzahler's way. Some little seed is beginning to sprout though, a night flower. Why haven't I heard from this brilliant young editor who has been assigned (is that the word?) my book? It's been a week. I bring out Smilin' Jack's image, how he looked that night in the bar of the restaurant. I hear his disembodied voice over the telephone. Will such a man bring me salvation from my woes?

There used to be a goddess of the night one could pray to—or stand (or lie) in fright of. The Greeks called her Nyx, the Romans Nox. She was born, together with Erebus (Darkness), Ge (Earth), and Eros (Love) out of Chaos. With Erebus she bore Aether (Upper Air) and Hemera (Day). By herself she spawned a large and generally unpleasant brood that included Moros (Doom), Thanatos (Death), Hypnos (Sleep), the Fates, and Nemesis.

In bygone religions light stood for the good, the healing time —night was the equivalent of evil or death. In ancient Egypt night was the time when the sun fought his daily battle with Apepi, the Serpent, and won to rise again in the east. In Genesis the original state of things was darkness. God created light. In folklore night is the time for demons, devils, hags and witches. During the light of day things are more or less normal.

When the new day is special, it often begins the night before. Twenty-four hours are not enough. Christmas Eve is an example. And Halloween comes the night before All Hallows Day. The Jewish Sabbath begins with darkness on the eve of the seventh day. Night is when, according to old wives' tales, baby snatching takes place. Lights blaze in the room of an unbaptized or uncircumcised child lest an evil-bent spirit take the infant, leaving a changeling in its place. Legends say disease-causing demons rove the night and, until recent scientific study suggested otherwise, bedroom windows were kept closed at night to prevent these spirits from getting into sleeping chambers.

Somehow prayer is important before sleep. A safe sleep is a journey one must ask the Almighty for. The Babylonians called on Shamash, Sin, Nergal and Ninib. The Irish call on Mary, Joseph, Brigit and Patrick. A folk myth says that if you say "rabbit" out loud before going to sleep and the first thing when you awake, you will have a lucky month. (It doesn't work.)

Incubus is the evil spirit that comes in the night to copulate with the most pure and innocent virgin. Incubus is a nightmare. Werewolves and vampires also strike in the dark hours. A gentleman by day turns into a howling beast by the light of the moon. In a few legends, those of marriage tales, an animal through the day will transform itself into a man or charming prince at night.

Among savages (as among the more cosmopolitan) there is a widespread fear of the darkness. Many primitive people refuse to travel or even leave their huts or campfires at night; if they do, they arm themselves with torches and the like to keep evil spirits at bay since these fear the light. (Vampires fear the Cross.) Thus we find magical rites to overcome the terror of darkness. In New Caledonia a priest keeps a pot of dyed-black water handy before him when cutting the umbilical cord of a just-born boy. This insures that the boy will not fear the dark when he grows up.

The ancient Chinese broke all life and existence down into two camps, the dark and the light. Yin is darkness, yang light. The Sukai tribes believe that the lord of hell, who lives in the interior of the earth, is a friend of darkness and cannot bear the light. In Norse mythology Night and Day are mother and son, set in the sky by All-Father, who gives each a horse and chariot to drive around the earth. The White Mountain Apache believed that in the beginning there was no darkness, only light. Then came Badger who carried a basket. He gave it to Coyote with the warning that it not be undone. Coyote disobeyed and let out the night forever. . . .

I once rode shotgun on a long-distance truck across the country. The arrangement was made by Melvin Shestack, surely one of the most notable but unrecognized (by the general public) figures on the New York media circuit. When he was entertainment editor at the old *Saturday Evening Post,* he assigned me an article on a beautiful young starlet of whom great things were expected. I was flown to England and Hollywood and all expenses were paid. The starlet was poor Sharon Tate, a couple of years before she was murdered. At *True* magazine he sent me to live for a week on an oil barge in the Gulf of Mexico. Mel has a ballooning gray beard, eyes that dart and a distinctive walk: he seems to be pitching forward on his toes. I've heard that some writers have been sent by Shestack on missions dreamed up in his cranium and not exactly approved by the outlet he represented. There are tales of people calling heartbreakingly from places such as Katmandu and asking why the promised advance money hadn't arrived, mystifying manuscripts arriving long after Shestack had fled the coop and that no one else knew anything about, halls filled with debt collectors at every spot he ever worked. But he always bounces back, strong and resilient as ever. Nothing stops him. He is known in the trade as a top "idea man." *Playboy* hired him for a season to do nothing else but think up ideas for stories and to pick out a performer just before that performer made a big name for himself.

Melvin Shestack has always come through for me. No matter where he works or will ever work, I know that he will have a job or an assignment perking on the front burner for me. If he becomes President I can count on being Secretary of State. He thought up my sitting beside a long-distance trucker on an ordinary run. He tried various trucking firms with no luck, and finally had to settle on a moving van—a rig that transported household goods from one city to another. He located a trucker in New Jersey named Looney. Looney picked up goods from families along the East Coast and deposited them out West at towns where the people were moving. I was much younger then; I was unmarried. I got my hair cut, put on a windbreaker, packed a toilet kit and took a bus to New Jersey. Looney was getting ready to pull out in the dead of night.

Who hasn't wondered about the faceless drivers of those behemoths on the highways, men who careen downhill in a light whine and shift grinding gears going up? It seems a romantic way to earn your keep—no set hours, an endless stretch of highway before you. No boss over your shoulder. You could play music in the cockpit, have adventures in strange towns and be a member of a generally tough breed. Truckers stuck together but ultimately went their own way as loners. That was the story. Did they take pills? Did they have women in various towns or know the really great whorehouses of the land? Were they mean sons of bitches? Did they really intend to scare the bejesus out of you when they edged a hair away from the rear of your miserable VW bug on the low road into the valley? Were they kind—stopping to put out a brush fire, help a grandpa fix a flat, give directions to a lost tourist? Most importantly, could they get a full squint down into cars with female drivers who had their skirts hiked up?

Looney bore a striking resemblance to Nelson Algren. He had those scrawny legs and arms and a comfortable belly the size of a bowling ball. He had sharp features, a sudden stare and hair going thin and gray on top. He was living with a good-humored woman with soft curves and dimpled cheeks. She told me, the minute he was out of earshot, "Mike is one hell of a guy. He's incorruptible, and that's what always gets him in trouble. He was laid off as a policeman around here because he enforced the law. That's why he took up truck driving. To get away from people. Oh, a hell of a fellow he is."

We weren't due to pull out until four in the morning, and I was allowed to catch shut-eye on the living room couch while he and the woman bedded down elsewhere. A minute before the alarm sounded the woman's black cat leaped onto my chest and I sprang up screaming. Looney must not have liked my momentary loss of self-control. He didn't chuckle. He aimed a dissatisfied expression my way through our trip, as if I might not be quite up to snuff. It was dark and slightly wet as we climbed aboard the large red and white tractor-trailer parked out front. "One thing I want to tell you," he said before igniting the spark that sent the truck roaring, "is for you not to block my vision out your window. I got to look in the rearview mirror out there. Just don't lean forward."

The headlights glowed and a red light blinked on the dash. We left in a hiss of hydraulic brakes and the deep rumble of the motor. Into a dark that gradually turned into a gray dawn. I was excited high up in the cab, turning this way and that. Looney sat on a pneumatic seat which took the bumps with oiled precision. I felt every one of them. I tried the radio and found it didn't work; Looney forgot when it had stopped working. He offered me some coffee out of a thermos and I spilled a quarter of a cup down my leg. He then grumpily taught me a truck driver's trick: Never fill a cup more than half full. I marveled at the way his hand flew up and down on the gear lever. It was almost constantly going. I started to tell him of my admiration, squirming around, when he barked, "Didn't I tell you! Back, back! I can't see nothing!"

I was with Looney for six days and nights. I learned a lot. I learned that he took no interest in politics, in movies, in books. He wore Jockey shorts. He claimed he thought of nothing, zero, as he tooled along—no fantasies, no plans, nothing. He said it was hard enough just driving the rig without having to think, too. Driving over long periods had caused him to come down with the piles. He took no pills, no dope, just coffee. He didn't care what the scenery was outside. He didn't marvel at the broad Texas sky at night with the millions of stars above or a flat moon-raked road ahead.

Long-haul truckers, Looney included, prefer the nights for driving. Cars drop off, the temperature falls in scorching months, and the Law is not apt to be around as much. Night is when you can really floorboard it, lean back and let the cool air whip in and not have to worry about traffic jams and clots of automobiles. Just space to get over, timeless. Looney got irritated when something broke his rhythm. We pulled into a truck stop late one night, and Looney took me to an inconspicuous annex behind it which had rough-lumber siding. There was a lot of beer being swigged and loud, raucous country music played. From the look of some of the rouged-cheeked sweetmeats inside, the members might have included more than one hooker. It wasn't a coffee-swilling rest stop. It was somewhere on the road in the middle of nowhere. Looney wouldn't have a beer. ("Might foul up my driving. But you go ahead.") Some of the other truckers weren't considering putting on the brakes. They were whooping and shaking a leg as if there were no tomorrow. Looney couldn't wait to get back on the road and fall into a kind of bug-eyed state. But when we got back to the trailer-truck we found the huge rear wheels had sunk down in mud. We were stuck and no one was around to pull us out. I heard Looney curse for the first time: "Goddamn my ass back to Jersey!"

Looney decided we should bed down in the truck stop for a few hours and get a wrecker company at first light to get us moving again. We took twin beds in a small, plywood-paneled room with a plastic motif. The mattresses were foam rubber. I have a lasting memory of Looney sitting on the edge of his bed, munching a ham and cheese sandwich in his Jockey shorts, staring at the floor the same way he looked out at the road from

the cab of his truck. After a while he flipped himself over between the sheets. I don't know how long we slept—not long—
for Looney seemed to be up no sooner than I shut my eyes,
dressed, hair wet-combed, and ready to trot. I was amazed by
how quickly and effortlessly the huge behemoth was plucked
from the mud by an ordinary-sized wrecker. Nothing to it. We
were back on the road.

At every town we entered, whether to load or drop off, a
would-be helper would spy us from an open window and come
running. "Hey, mister, need a hand?" They were usually boys,
mostly black, and they popped up at the crack of dawn as the
powerful truck shattered the early morning quiet of sleepy
little towns. "Hey, mister, I'm strong. I can last. Let me do it."
They would swing on the cab door or hurtle themselves
through the cab window. Occasionally there would be fights to
see who would be chosen; Looney seemed to encourage that
method of selection. I was taken as a common laborer myself
and to be considered one came as a rude shock—no matter if I
had told Looney that I wanted to pass myself off as a helper, not
a writer. For verisimilitude, you see. One tall black boy thought
he had a right to my seat in the cab. "You, man, been sitting long
enough. Let me have it a while." We struggled, and it was the
one time Looney laughed and seemed to get a kick out of the
trip.

In a daze I helped load household goods. One job was an army
sergeant's family, moving from an eastern to a western base.
There were bowling balls and gimcracks and broken furniture
and plates. The house they left was a shambles, with kicked-out
screens and shattered windows. It smelled of stale beer, endless
fights and tired fornication. There was an immaculate, tidy
house which an old man and his wife were leaving for the sun of
New Mexico. The man had a hobby—model trains; only his
prized train came as close to the real thing, a giant, gleaming
array of cars and engine painted cheery circus colors. It ran on
steam and required ten strong men, all grunting, wheezing and
cursing, to shove it up the truck ramp. The little old man ran
around, wringing his hands: "Watch the sides now! I don't want
to interfere, but those wheels are delicate. They're set to milli-

meters. The least jar will make them not fit the track. Excuse me, pardon me—please, please watch it!"

Looney fit tracks and all inside the truck with the economy of a surgeon. Nearly whole towns disappeared in that truck. Looney threw rope knots and gray quilts left and right, stuffing here, plugging up there, making gigantic households boil down to midget size the way a wrecked car goes through a pulverizing machine in a junkyard and comes out the dimensions of a steamer trunk. He did it grumpily, his Nelson Algren, skinny-shanked body flitting around the interior of the trailer-truck in a sweat. As the miles increased, he more and more fell into his stance of being Boss, with me as his nincompoop Laborer. Along about Texas he forgot entirely that I was a writer who did stories. He began teaching me arcane methods of storage and removal in the truck as if I were learning an occupation. He got terribly exasperated when I didn't throw a quilt right or not carry five objects when three were weighing me down. "Get moving—we haven't all day."

During the day, we did the loading and unloading, the hard, backbreaking work. Nights were for driving. I slept when I felt like it in the minibed behind the cab seat. It had a little curtain. The mattress was hard and I had to bend my legs to fit. I dozed off hearing the grinding of gears and awoke with them, the sudden acceleration and braking tossing me around like a rag doll. I slept while my arms flopped and my back vibrated. Looney hardly ever slept. He took a few hours shut-eye every now and then in a truck-stop cubicle along the way—but it always seemed more an afterthought than a necessity. He pulled into a stop in Knoxville and said, "OK," which meant we would stretch out on beds there for three hours and then be off. I had gone to college in Knoxville, but that fact seemed irrelevant. I wasn't going to call anybody there or visit landmarks. Looney seemed no more refreshed afterward than before.

I observed truckers at these rest stops. None appeared healthy. Big, full bellies were much in evidence, also thin legs and dazed, half-mad, eccentric looks. They liked to believe that they belonged to a fraternity—and expected little perks from it. Coffee was supposed to be waved under their noses the minute they sat on truck-stop stools. They flicked their lights at one another on the road. They beeped their horns in secret codes to warn each other that a highway patrol car lay in speed-trap ambush down the road. They stopped to help when one of their brotherhood had pulled off with a busted axle or a flat or any kind of malaise. They swapped yarns and winked at the waitresses and behaved no differently in Richmond than Albuquerque. It was all one endless road. I remember sitting in a toilet stall next to one sheltering a woebegone trucker. The heels of his cowboy boots were worn down, the ends of his denim trousers ragged and mud-caked. He groaned, a low, long-standing whelp of anguish. He came out buckling his belt over a king-sized belly, his T-shirt stretched to the ripping point. "It's a son-of-a-bitching life, ain't she, buddy," he said, to me and the four walls. "I haven't been able to shit in five days."

Night on the road was when the world stopped. We drove through the vastness of Texas with a giant spread of stars above. It had rained a short time before and cool, gentle air came in the windows. I sat deep in my seat and watched the heavens and wondered, never daring to share the sentiment with Looney, if somewhere in those millions of pinpoints of light another life was being lived. Why not? The truck tickled the small of my back like someone shaking me awake. Maybe the heavens and earth are no bigger than molecules and atoms in our own bodies. Maybe this planet, on which Looney was wheeling his rig, is no larger than some atom in my body in the scheme of things, in the eternity of Time. In reaches beyond ours there would be no day or night. All the scurrying about we do on this globe would have no more ultimate consequence than the flurry of cockroaches caught at 3 A.M. in sudden electric light. Our Civil War would hardly make a rustle. Henry Kissinger would hardly loom large.

On the way to El Paso we drove parallel, on a modern interstate, to a narrow tarmac road that was no longer in use. Weeds sprouted from its cracks and parts of it were covered by dust. That was the road I had taken a couple of decades before when I was twenty-three and a member of the oddball group of writers James Jones and Lowney Handy had assembled. I was on my way to Tucson, with a detour through El Paso, to see my two mentors when I had traveled that tarmac which was now sprouting weeds and holding dust. It had seemed a large road then, how a state road leading to an important city should look. I was in love with a girl back in Tennessee but was denying it in order to follow a romantic conception of what a writer and artist should be—unencumbered and rolling along. I felt when I sat up high with Looney that I should acknowledge somehow that I had been on the other road one time, that life had been totally different then. "Did you ever take that other road over there?" I asked Looney.

"No."

"I did once. I remember seeing a tiny speck of light on the horizon. It kept getting larger and larger. It became El Paso. That's something, isn't it, the way you see a city far off on the horizon out West and travel hundreds of miles before you get there?"

"Yep."

"Wonder when that other road stopped being used?"

"I don't know."

There was no time for reflection in the day. The world entered. One family we moved had a squadron of teenagers. I would come around a corner in a nearly stripped bedroom and find a couple wrapped around each other, barely breaking stride for me. I moved generally as an invisible person, a laborer whose presence didn't count. I wasn't a father, a potential lover, a friend, a soul mate, a human being. What did it matter what I saw? This household—and most—didn't offer coffee or any treat. We had to ask for water, and glasses were carefully washed after we drank. Happily I was slipped a five-spot now and then—a tip—when the last smelly rug, the final broken cup was fitted into the bursting-at-the-seams truck. "This is for you, sonny."

"Thank you very much."

"And make sure now that those bowling balls are not scratched when you lift them out. They are Herbert's pride and joy. He will kill us if they get scarred."

Heat and people and problem solving were features of the day. Early one morning we tooled up before the retirement villa in Carlsbad of the old gentleman with the train. He had flown in before us. He was up and clapping his hands at his door, waiting for his stupendous train to come rolling in. It was too much for Looney and me to manage on our own.

"Now don't let Pappa help you," the missus told us sotto voce. "He'll just hurt himself if he tries. You know how excitable he gets."

My judgment was that if the old lady hadn't spoken up, Looney wouldn't have minded the old retiree's help. We drove into Carlsbad for the usual gaggle of helpers, but this one time none showed. No one ran to greet us. We went to a bar at around eight in the morning where already there was a scattering of customers ensconced. A tired-looking musician sat slumped on a raised platform at one end of the bar, electronic cords and amplifiers around him. Chrome flashed from his musical paraphernalia. The bartender was a woman who wore tight twill trousers and a pearl-studded Western shirt. She was in a very cheerful mood, considering the clientele and the time of day. A high-velocity wind was rattling windows and signs on the street outside, and it howled in the front door whenever a new face appeared. I took a Coor's and felt a secret, private joy. When you drive through the night, you are allowed a cold beer in the morning.

We were among working people and soon met Glenn, a slow-smiling man with wavy hair and friendly eyes. He told us he had been laid off from the mines after working there ten years, didn't know where his next nickel was coming from and didn't care. He was from the South, my neck of the woods, and had come to Carlsbad because he had heard there was good money in the mines. He drank his brew straight from the bottle. The musician on the platform broke out into *The Green, Green Grass of Home* as if on cue. The music in this kind of place had to do with doomed love and the longing for home. Every song was a hard-luck story. Every man jack in this place had a tale of woe to tell. No one was discussing deals or co-ops or Hampton vacations. Looney chimed in, saying he had a rig with a train on it and he can't get it down.

"A train? On a truck?" Glenn said. The kookiness of the idea appealed to him. He took a slug of beer. "I got a wrench on my pickup. I'll take it off for you."

"You ever take anything down that heavy?"

"Didn't I tell you I was a miner?" Glenn said. "I can take anything out that can come out."

He did. He stretched a heavy steel band around the train and brought it off slowly, his pickup bouncing up and down and seeming ready to strip a gear and fly apart. The effort took the entire morning and almost wrecked his pickup. He charged nothing. Glad to do it. Anytime. One working stiff helps out another. Besides, he got to prove he could do it. We could buy him a beer the next time we came through. The old man, with a frizz of white hair around a bald dome, winced and cried at every step. He began polishing his toy the moment it was docked in a barnlike garage. His wife found a broken teacup and a wobbly leg on the sofa we carted in, and Looney solemnly and importantly listed these items on a form he carried. ("They'll forget about it after a while," he told me later. "Seeing me write down something makes them feel better at the time. Nothing'll come of it.") The woman considered Looney management and did not tip him. She gave me the standard five bucks. "Here you are, boy." I decided to have a couple of drinks on her at the Lion's Head when I got back to New York and was in mufti.

We drove on. Who can figure out life and its convolutions? A while back in Tennessee I had taken in a movie with Gregory Peck and Tuesday Weld. Ralph Meeker was cast as Tuesday Weld's father, a redneck moonshiner in overalls and slouch hat. I'd always been a secret fan of Meeker's, have indelibly inscribed in my brain many of the parts he has played and have been both pleased by his scant celebrity and alarmed that it could happen to such a fine, competent actor. A few hours after the movie I caught a jet to New York and went to a bar on Madison Avenue to get my bearings back. Seated also in that bar, wearing a fine flannel suit and red suspenders, was Ralph Meeker. I don't know what the odds were that that would happen, but it happened. I saw him as a hillbilly on the screen in Tennessee. A moment later—thanks to the speed of jet travel— I encountered him in the flesh as a distingué gent on Madison Avenue.

Looney and I parted in Juárez, Mexico. He was going on to Los Angeles, I was flying back to New York to write my story.

We stood together our last time in a trucker's bar in Juárez, elbows down on the counter, Looney stoical as ever, myself punchy and trembling with exhaustion. It was well past midnight and the place was brimming with the bellies of truckers and a sea of sunburned necks passing to and fro. No authentic Mexicans seemed to be in evidence except for the help. Model trucks lined the top shelf behind the bar, and there were colored pictures of rigs, all showing that the place favored the trucking set. Conversations buzzed about what the Law was up to in various states concerning truckers. Recent wrecks were being detailed, physical ailments compared. Everyone was putting it away.

An incipient fight started a yard or two down the bar from us. A crew-cut fireplug had his fists doubled up, his sunburned neck turning a darker purplish shade. The other man—smooth black hair, nervous gestures, somewhat elegant—eyeballed him steadily and patiently explained that he was going to kill him if matters went further. A blast of lickety-split Mexican music broke from the jukebox, and both men edged closer. The door swung open, rays of neon from outside flashing, and two slicked-down, broadly grinning constabularies stepped in, guns and bullets and billies gleaming on their belts. The elegant trucker's words continued at the same pitch, but abruptly shifted gears in mid-sentence: ". . . cut your gizzard out and stuff—uh-oh, drop your hands and smile. Here come the boys, and if they land us we'll be in the poky for twenty years or ten grand. Don't fool around—*smile, smile, smile*. Shake my hand and laugh. Go on. They're getting closer." The two truckers broke into ear-to-ear grins, the fireplug seeming nearly to have to break a bone to do it. They shook hands and embraced. "How do you do, gentlemen," the elegant trucker said to the constabularies. "May we buy you a drink?" Offer accepted. The two beaming constabularies polished off a tequila, glancing around. Wherever their eyes struck, like a flashlight's glow, a trucker smiled and waved. When they left, the music was turned up a decibel and rodeo-type yelps were heard. The incipient fight was forgotten.

"You never want to get arrested here," Looney said in his usual meager choice of words. He didn't care to elaborate.

A friend of Looney's showed up, a trucker we'd last run across in Oklahoma. Truckers often run across each other at various spots on long-distance runs—truck stops, gas stations, weight stations and, in this case, a Mexican bar-cum-whorehouse. This place had a deep alcove of tables filled with bosomy perfumed-to-the-heavens ladies. They did not rise from the table unless they snagged a customer and took him into the warren of tiny, dimly lit rooms in back. Looney's friend—a tall, chuckling, loose-limbed Southerner—had the look of someone who had just been back there. He was relaxed. He told jokes. He kidded Looney. He seemed to be having fun—and would have fun, no matter where or what. He had a Road Runner emblem on the front of his truck, many tape decks inside, and twin silver air horns gleamed above his door ready to blast the road clear in front of him. Why couldn't I have been assigned him instead of Looney? Traveling with Looney was like traveling with Cotton Mather. Truckers were all different down deep, I realized.

Suddenly Looney had left his space at the bar. His friend and I swapped yarns, fed the juke and matched each other drink for drink. Now and then we wondered about Looney. "You think he's sick in the john maybe?" I said. "I haven't seen him back there though."

"He may be back there in the back eating it," his friend said.

When we stopped thinking about Looney, he showed up. No explanations, joy or tale to relate. The same tight-lipped reaction was probably there when he returned home after the month-long cross-country trek. He'd just walk in, put his thermos down, and turn on the TV. Didn't matter any more than going down to the corner for bread and a quart of milk. But maybe I had been locked together with him too long. We were both sick of each other. We bid adieu in the bar, and I caught a plane out that morning from El Paso. At dawn I'd seen a line of truckers hop in their cabs, rev up their motors and roll out. I'd been one of them that night, but now in the daylight of morning I rejoined my old life. Clerks were nicer to me: "Check your bag, sir?" Fellow passengers talked to me on the plane. I had a double scotch and soda and watched the sun's rays bounce off the plane's gray aluminum wings. Daylight.

Twelve

*At night we celebrate. Graduation night, University of Tennessee, Knoxville: Charley Hickerson and I decide to stay up as long as we can. We stay up sixty hours straight. No more exams, no job yet or hint of one. Lots of 7-Up and gin, pack after pack of cigarettes and a few cigars, charging across fields and part of the campus on rented horses and wearing derbies, and—crowning glory—hanging up a Budweiser reproduction of Custer's Last Stand (stolen from a beer joint) in the freshman girls' dorm. Take that, ladies! The joy to say, "I been drunk sixty hours straight with Charley." But I couldn't sleep when I finally lay down next to my rolled diploma. I read a new book I'd found—*From Here to Eternity—*on the sun deck of the ATO house. I went back to Johnson City in the daylight and ate three meals a day, went to bed early at night, watched my manners, and no one could have imagined what I had recently done through the night. Nor could I have ever imagined in my wildest dreams what waited in the future.*

A SHIVER—and when my hand goes in my pajamas, I feel a damp sweat over my chest. A trickle runs down my back. Smilin' Jack has turned down my book. I couldn't get him by phone; the word came coldly by mail. In the letter he said the two editors didn't have something called "commitment" toward it. First the young female editor, then a man whose name I didn't know from Adam. They had enthusiasm but not commitment. "Thanks, anyway, and I do hope you'll find that commitment elsewhere. The writing is good, the tone just right. Good wishes." I feel shame, shame that someone has stepped into my world, taken a good strong sniff and walked out. I feel hurt and wounded and worthless—*bothered and bewildered, am I. Be-witched, bothered and bewildered—am I!* I played *Pal Joey* over and over on the record player when I lived in Washington over twenty years ago and was at loose ends. I conjure up faces from there—as fresh as if a second ago.

The refrigerator keeps going on and off, through thick and thin, rejection and success. The beard still sprouts on my chin. . . . Try to sleep. Start relaxing your toes, then ankles . . . Goddamnit, *101 Uses for a Dead Cat* goes on the best-seller list! Rosemary Rogers writes blockbusters. *Real Men Don't Eat Quiche* is at the head of the pack. I begin, eyes shut, an op-ed piece for the *Times,* telling what it is to be on Grub Street today. I wonder in it why particular people chose the careers of publisher and editor and writer. What chemistry goes into their systems, what chances of luck and fortune have made them who they are? What do publishers dream about? As little boys and girls did they dream of one day bringing out Miss Piggy? . . . I turn my body and hear the report of a firecracker or firearm. How the bloody fuck am I supposed to get twenty-five hundred dollars to meet expenses? Fine and good to write an op-ed piece, a His'm (in lieu of a Hers), a *Village Voice* lament for love —but it takes real hard dollars to hold the fort. You have to pay the bills. There's school, American Express, rent . . . *Stop!* Don't think about it till tomorrow. . . . Think of Tennessee and green hills and . . .

I think of James T. Farrell and what he told me when I came to interview him during his last days at the Beaux Arts Hotel in New York. He wore thick-lensed glasses and had steel-gray hair and was somewhat stooped. He walked around in his tiny, cluttered apartment in his stocking feet, plucking yellowing manuscripts from under books, out of drawers and off shelves. He talked and ate writing. He could hardly stop writing to talk to me. He may have been a little balmy during that final stretch before the grave. He told me he wasn't finished, that the time hadn't arrived to count James T. Farrell out yet. He suddenly streaked across the room, leaped in the air and kicked both stockinged feet against the wall. "Anybody who can do that can't be counted out."

He wrote through the night. He wrote until his fingers were

bloody. There were people out there who were James T. Farrell readers. They still bought his books. But reviewers didn't pay serious attention during his final years. He had always had trouble with publishers, he told me. Near the end of our talk, my interview, he kept looking over at his desk. Work beckoned. Either that or the glance was toward a calling card for a pizza joint that was thumbtacked to the wall. He might have been getting hungry. I asked him what awaited James T. Farrell in the future, where was he heading. "Don't tell anyone," he said. "It's a secret, but I'm a shoo-in for the Nobel Prize. I'm going to get it. Hubert Humphrey told me so."

"Is there anything you would have done differently in your career? Do you have any regrets?"

"I have one regret and one great wish," he said in his rapid speech, in his mock-serious tone. "They are the same, my regret and my wish. I wish I'd had every publisher in the world in one room—one large, cozy room with one door. I'd lock that door. But before I'd lock that door I'd toss in a goddamn bomb. I regret I didn't get to do it. I wish I had. . . ."

Wind rattles my window. I think of Farrell quite often, once a month at least. It's been over fifteen years since I saw him in that well-lived-in hotel-room-cum-apartment. He was living his last moments there. Night was falling. *Studs Lonigan* had long since become a classic. . . . Pellets of rain strike the window in my apartment in short bursts. . . . Think of the black nights your father must have gone through in the heart of the Depression. It won't bear thinking about. . . . The boys have pj's from Bloomie's, pj's with football numbers on them and elastic at the ankles and wrists. Forget it's a charge; they're wearing them. In Tennessee when you were their age, you wore a cut-down shirt of your father's as a nightgown. . . . We'll get through. We'll work through this night the way we have all the others. My God, remember those nights in Tennessee during adolescence when you couldn't sleep? You kept reminding yourself you were falling asleep every time you began falling asleep. That tic in the nervous system kept you awake. It was a problem you couldn't explain to anyone. Wet dreams were going off like firecrackers. You lived through that. . . . Seems so quaint now.

I pull the sheet over my head, draw my knees up and thank

God I'm not back in Korea. Every time it's cold and damp and raining and night and I have a bed to lie in, I know that no matter what awfulness I'm in or what awaits me, nothing can ever again quite equal Korea. To have once been on guard duty at night when it was fifteen below zero in Korea gives one a sense of proportion that lasts through life.

I had just turned eighteen when I joined the Army in 1946. I had never been further west than Chattanooga. In three months' time, after basic training at Fort Knox, I boarded the *Marine Dragon* in San Francisco for the long ride to Inchon, Korea. When my destination had been called out in the repo depo, I didn't know where Korea actually was. The Caribbean? Somewhere near the Philippines? I hardly shaved back then, had only known one woman carnally and ever so briefly. I weighed 128 pounds and stood six feet two inches tall. I had never been on a ship. I had never seen an ocean wave. We sailed out of San Francisco past the Golden Gate into the night, gradually leaving a shoreline filled with bright, twinkling lights behind. On the dark ocean we felt the first roll of the ship beneath our feet. We sailed by way of the Aleutians in the wake of a tidal wave. I arose chipper my first morning at sea, peeling off from one slab in a tier of bunks to brush my teeth. I was from a good home in Tennessee and had been taught to brush my teeth.

In the head a strange sight awaited me. Over nearly every bowl, with water gushing continuously down it, a head hung. Deep, guttural cries and thin puke came from downturned mouths. All had passed beyond shame. The ship leaped in the air, came down with a crash, and listed back and forth to the sides. The cries came as the ship rose and sank. I took one look, dropped my toothbrush and began vomiting with the best of them. I stayed there all that day and through the night, hanging onto a bowl. Finally a light greenish fluid came out—bile, I was told later. Messages came over the squawk box, all disregarded: *"Now hear this, now hear this—Private John Bowers, RA14218267, report on the double to C deck. If you don't you will be marked AWOL."* I never reported anywhere. I only wished I could die. At last I was able to discern graffiti by my bowl, with its ever flowing stream, and knew I was going to make it. I could smile.

> I have shit on the banks of the Wabash,
> I have shit over Niagara Falls,
> But this is the first time I ever sat down to shit
> And at the same time watered my balls.

Three days after making it back to my bunk, with vomit raining down from someone above, someone unable to make it to the head, I became ravenously hungry. No hunger have I ever known like that—not for fame nor sex nor water. We were fed slop, or something bordering on slop, two times a day. It was served in a galley reeking of disinfectants. It was a yellowish-green square of a rubbery substance—too hard for powdered eggs, although that might have been in it. It never varied. The second meal was gooey, sharp and rancid-scented. It was covered by a white paste and I never discovered what it was. I could only get down a couple of mouthfuls before I started moving toward the head and a toilet bowl.

I dreamed of food. I cursed myself for the times I had had peanut butter sandwiches available, gallons of fresh milk to wash it down with at home, and hadn't taken advantage of them. I made up fantasies about food the way I had done with sex and a high school teacher. I pictured a casual meeting with a bowl of spaghetti, a baloney sandwich introduced to me, a roast I'd run across. Such fetching morsels, so saucy and appetizing. All of us dogfaces were starving. The braver ones began patrols into the officers' quarters and the Merchant Marine section. Military training, such as it was, was coming in handy. They came back with tales of pungent slices of red ham, fresh fried eggs, sugar buns and apple bins. They were like sex yarns that in the bottom of one's heart one doesn't believe, yet are so irresistible and satisfy such a need that one throws incredulity to the wind.

Then one late afternoon as a squad or two of us loafed about topside, gazing at rolling sea and water as far as the eye could see, some Merchant Marines came out of a hatch in their black knitted watch caps and blue denim shirts. They were laughing. They took plates of fried chicken, leftovers from their meal, and began throwing the crispy golden-brown meat on the gray iron deck. We fought for pieces, fists flying and feet slipping out from under us. I got a wishbone from under someone's heel and sucked the meat off in a couple of gulps. The Merchants were in great high humor, throwing food to far corners, high in the air, to see who could race faster, to find out how much sport they could make of it. We lost our embarrassment—there was none actually—just as we abandoned shame when we threw up our bile in the head. Nothing mattered but a piece of chicken and our empty guts. The Merchants laughed wildly and we did, too, as the sun began falling. It was 1946 and the U.S.A. had won the war.

The Russians occupied the northern half of Korea, above the 42nd Parallel; we took over the bottom half. It was the most brutalized, godforsaken spit of land I ever saw. My battalion stayed first in an abandoned Japanese factory. It was a huge concrete structure with dingy glass skylights far up and permitting few sun rays. It was damp and dank and cold and bunks were lined up in many rows from one end to the other. It looked like the wounded lined up in *Gone With the Wind* without the heat of Atlanta. Next we moved into flimsy prefab buildings that had a couple of oil stoves in the center which always died out during the night. By then winter had set in in force. I was never warm. I quoted "Sam McGee from Tennessee" to myself like a litany. I slept with all my clothes on, boots and all, my ration of blankets pulled over my head. I wrote home for blankets and comforters. My mother couldn't understand or thought it was a joke. I was in the American Army. I became hungry again—all of us did. Food shipments had become fouled up and our outfit received a ton of chicken from Australia as our only meat supply. We were drowning in chicken. We had chicken fricassee, chicken casserole, chicken a la king (a big favorite)—all ways of preparing chicken that didn't let one visualize it as chicken. No fried chicken. The frozen chickens from Australia could not stand up to frying, no way to shape them and distinguish a leg from the pope's nose, as you couldn't get a fried egg from powdered eggs (also on the menu). My mother couldn't understand how I could be in the U.S. Army and need food shipped;

again, a joke of some sort. I stayed hungry and I stayed cold. But I kept brushing my teeth.

However, no misery quite equaled guard duty at night in Korea. We had inspection at twilight and then were hauled off to various strategic locations to stand guard with our M1's through the long night. We were inspected by the officer of the guard for haircut trim, shaved cheeks, the polish on boots and the cleanliness of shirts and ties under hooded parkas—and then taken by an olive-drab two-and-a-half to protect some kind of storage depot. We were dropped off singly, one by one, at our posts. I never knew what I was guarding or who might attack. It was four hours on, four hours off. Deep in the night I lay in the guard's shack on a cot, bundled up in my parka, cradling my M1. Someone would whack my boot. "OK, Mac, you go out now." By flashlight I climbed aboard a rumbling two-and-a-half. When everyone was aboard, the backflap went up on the truck and we bounced off. Every road was pockmarked by craters and we rolled from side to side. On the way we listened to yarns by veterans about an unfortunate who had recently had his balls cut off while standing guard. "The gooks are getting back at us. I ain't losing my balls though. They got to shoot me in the heart first."

Dropped off then in some pitch-black spot or by a klieg-lit barbed-wire compound, into a narrow shack or by a gravel pit. The truck roared off. Snow was sometimes falling. It became very still in the moments after the truck's roar died away. A snowflake would land on my eyelash and freeze. Most often it was too cold to snow. But I stood there with my M1, trying to do what I had been told to do—keep rifle at sling arms, bring it to port and throw a shell in the chamber when challenging a noise or someone. I kept repeating my one command under my breath, "Halt, who goes there!" If someone said, "Friend," I was to say, "Pass and be recognized." The dialogue must have been thought up for Corregidor or some hot climate. My tongue was nearly frozen. After thirty minutes I couldn't walk. I stood there in the dark, moving my trigger finger to see if it still worked, and wondered what I was doing in this predicament halfway around the world from where I had started out. Only months before I had been trying out for the high school basketball team and agonizing over a girl who scarcely knew I existed. I had never been afraid of anyone except a grammar-school teacher who wore thick glasses. I had volunteered for the Army because I had seen servicemen come home heroes in uniform during the Second World War. My older brother Howard had worn the grand white of a naval officer and had no problem with girls. Now I held an M1 and was freezing.

A red-nosed captain with bow legs, officer of the guard, came up in a jeep. He went by the book, a stickler for rules. He was an ex-enlisted man. We glanced askance at each other in the moonlight while he disembarked from the jeep. "Halt, who goes there," I screamed in a shrill voice. He replied calmly that he was Captain So-and-So. I had slammed a shell in the M1 chamber—regulations—only because I feared he would reprimand me if I hadn't. My finger was around the trigger. Fumbling, numb with cold, I could have shot him. He was probably as close to death as he'd ever been in the service. He calmly inspected the rifle, asked me if I'd heard any suspicious noises, seen anything. All was well. He drove off in his jeep.

The two-and-a-half that was to bring my replacement had broken down. The night air became sharper. I could barely move my legs. I couldn't bring my rifle up to port if trouble did arise. The wind howled around corners bringing the ordure of a honey cart. Finally I could hear the two-and-a-half in the far distance, a promise. I could have wept for joy if my eyes had worked. It roared up in a blaze of headlights. My replacement was pushed off and two men began lifting me aboard. Apparently they had been facing this problem down the road with others. We were too frozen to move, blocks of ice. "What the hell happened? How come you're so late?" "Trucks breaking down in this fucking cold. Nothing is moving." We got back to our area in a gritty dawn. There would be no shower to take and warm up (there was none), no food except coffee and doughnuts from an incongruous Red Cross shack with a Red Cross woman. Nights passed like that on guard duty in Korea. Others have had far worse nights elsewhere—but for years guard duty in the cold in Korea served as a barometer for me for what the human body and spirit can endure and survive.

On free nights we went into Seoul on passes. My first night

there, to see a movie, I got lost from the battalion truck. I was alone and lost halfway around the world. I was racing down narrow, winding streets shouting, "Forty-second Engineers. Anybody from the Forty-second?" Squatting Koreans looked at me with large, solemn eyes, unblinking. Finally a huge black soldier behind the wheel of a two-and-a-half said, "Where you going?"

"Yong Dong Po."

"Hop in, Mac. You just made the last motherfucker going out tonight."

I crawled in the two-and-a-half's dark cavern of a truck bed. I could only guess by their accents who might be sharing space with me—a slow drawl from someone beside me, a black guy's hearty comments down the bench, a Brooklyn staccato speech across the aisle. Everyone was talking pussy and hating the gooks. The driver sped over a rutted, dusty road. Outside passed a landscape of rice paddies in the moonlight and shacks with unshaded light bulbs burning hotly. Now and then we roared past a bicyclist or a creaking, rusting, groaning jalopy. Many Koreans, particularly the young, wore olive-drab GI clothing—fatigues and boots. The Japanese uniforms they had pilfered became less evident each day.

There came into view a Korean patriarch on a bicycle. He wore white with one of those tall black tubular hats that distinguished the wise in that land. He was peddling away with feet in black slippers, impervious to our existence. (The country had been occupied since time immemorial; he realized invaders came and went.) He didn't look our way as we whooshed past. But suddenly an enormous crater faced our driver and he slowed to inch around it. "Hey, granddad, wud you doing on this road? Got a daughter we can fuck?"

He was peddling along in the moonlight, not turning his head. He couldn't understand the words. He kept his back ramrod straight. Someone from the truck took a stone and whipped it at the old man. It sailed past. Another GI stood. I thought at first he was going to reprimand the first one. Instead he held a stone himself. He flung it and knocked the old man's tall black hat off. The old man looked at us all, in the moonlight, with startled, terrorized eyes. "I got him the first motherfuck throw. How you like that?"

I still see the eyes of that old man in the moonlight over thirty years later. When I first heard of troops going to Vietnam during the Kennedy years, I knew it was wrong. I wasn't in a think tank or dean of students at Harvard, but I knew it was wrong. I knew it was wrong through the Johnson years and the reign of Dr. Kissinger. There were other nights in Korea. I watched an ROK officer, a Korean with bright, rosy cheeks, beat a fellow Korean in a guard shack. The captured Korean had been apprehended while stealing. His moon face was pitted from a long-ago attack of smallpox and was a waxy color. The ROK officer spewed out a stream of invective in Korean at the man, spittle flying, and then he brought a stanchion down on the side of the man's head and his shoulder. He really hit him. The man whimpered, then turned and giggly-grinned through broken teeth at the Americans. Sorry this has to be done in front of you, he seemed to say, but it has to be. It's how we do things here. I got caught, but I can take it. The ROK officer smiled, too. Everybody smiled. The side of the man's head was swelling like a balloon and his shoulder seemed broken.

Another night I picked up a Miss Kim in the Bung Chung Dance Hall in downtown Seoul. Every woman in Korea seemed to be named Kim. She flirted with me, giggled, and stroked my arm. No female in Johnson City, Tennessee, had ever done that. The dance hall was festooned with the colored lights of Christmas, and dour Russians and American GI's dallied inside. A thirty-second-long dance cost a string of tickets, and no matter how many you purchased in advance at the door, they soon ran out. Miss Kim could speak but one or two words of English, and she wore the traditional long white skirt with a wide black sash. She let me know by sign language, a giggly nod and most of her English words that I was welcome to spend the night with her. No one had ever made that proposition to me before. I felt I was suddenly in the middle of a novel. I was flattered, and I was powerless. I followed. No man walked with a woman on the street in Korea. Miss Kim motioned for me to stay a discreet block behind her as she wound her way through back alleys and down dusty paths. The world smelled of garlic and honey carts and acrid smoke. No evidence of Americans anywhere. I was being swallowed up in the heart of Korea, in the night. I couldn't turn back because I didn't know where I was, or exactly what I was turning back from.

Miss Kim let me in a side door to a small, bare room. Light from the narrow, deserted street filtered in through the paper windows, and I watched Miss Kim take two sleeping pallets from somewhere and spread them on the matted floor. She took off her clothes and I followed suit, but, for some atavistic urge to prepare for possible flight, I kept my boots on. We must have made some sight. Miss Kim was nut-brown and lovely in the dim, shadowy light, far more solemn now than she had been in the Bung Chung Dance Hall. She put her fingers to her lips to tell me to be absolutely silent. I didn't mind. I didn't want to upset any neighbors. Now what? She removed some bills from my wallet, giggled and nodded, and put them in a secret hiding place.

I moved to kiss her, but she would have none of that. She had ceased stroking my arm, too. Her eyes looked sad and wary. Every time I made a move for her she put a finger to her lips and pointed to an adjacent room. I gathered after a while that in the next room slept her father or brother—husband?—and that he would cut off my pecker if he found us together. In sign language she apprised me of this fact, using her finger to simulate a knife and drawing it near my member. She would not touch it. She would not touch me. We spent the night on pallets, side by side, my head on a small, brick-hard bolster. I listened bug-eyed all night for sounds from the room next door. But I heard nothing. I left at first light and immediately ran across a two-and-a-half barreling for Yong Dong Po. Miss Kim told me through her various means to come back and see her some time. I never did.

A Korean produce market is around the corner now on Sixth Avenue. It stays open late to catch those in need of a carton of milk or a Granny Smith apple. Balducci's and all others have lowered their metal gates. The Koreans are still hungry and out to satisfy. All the Koreans are spick-and-span, cheerful mostly, and deadly efficient. They wear bright polyester, jaunty caps and American designer jeans. They never seem tired or without something to do. Nights are when they do their big business. My favorite is a wasp-thin young woman in the latest fashion, her coal-black hair long and glistening, her eyes alert and superbly healthy. She makes jokes and talks in American slang. Often I'm tempted to say a few words in Korean and mention Yong Dong Po and Seoul. But I don't.

One thought strikes me as I lay awake at three o'clock in the middle of Manhattan Island. I am a lark. I was born to sleep in the dark. Why does my mind race so, keeping me up when my body says sleep? I should thank my stars though that I'm not out there working. Jocelyn is. She is the mother of Yasunari, who was in kindergarten with Nick. She is in the mother's circle and she works nights. From midnight until 8 A.M., five days a week, she answers phones for Pan Am, taking reservations and giving out information on fares. She has been doing it for three years and she says she likes it. She needs no baby-sitter for Yasunari, for he's at school from nine until three, when she sleeps. She is with her husband, Louis, through the evening until she leaves for work at twelve. It doesn't look bad on paper. She has told me: "It's like not working in a way. It's a private time, being able to leave home and go off in the night. And the very, very best part of it is that when I'm coming home, work done, I see all these others going off to their day jobs. I feel lucky." But there is another side: "I'm always tired at night. It's like having a permanent hangover. Your body never really ever gets accustomed to working nights. People just aren't nocturnal animals. We need the light and a day rhythm to our lives or we suffer. Men have it easier who work nights. They don't have to do housework in addition to everything else." She told me finally, "To work nights you have to be adaptable. And no matter what the advantages, you miss daylight."

The first sentence in a book on astronomy in the Jefferson Market Library in Greenwich Village reads, "The sun is a star." Someone has scribbled beside it, "No, a Superstar!"
The sun is 109 times the diameter of earth and around 93 million miles away. Copernicus believed that the sun was cen-

tral in the heavens. It was not until the nineteenth century that the sun was put in its rightful place as one of a limitless number. Our sun is one of billions of stars in the Milky Way galaxy and the Milky Way is but one of billions of galaxies out there. We count stars and galaxies by the billions, but even so only a fraction of available space is being used. As big as each star is individually, there is great space between them. The stars we see at night are spread more thinly than a collection of golf balls spaced a hundred miles apart. We know (or think we know) what's out there by light waves and radio waves. Light waves travel at 186,000 miles per second, and sunshine takes eight seconds to reach Earth, moonlight a little over a second. Light from the nearer stars takes four years getting here. Light from the far ones takes forever. There are stars whose light started our way when Egyptians were building the pyramids and is just now reaching us.

The moon—our night beacon—pulls at the tide. It brings out werewolves and lights up the Headless Horseman. It is some 238,857 miles away, slightly more than a quarter of the diameter of the earth, and men have set foot on it. The moon of course revolves around the earth and has its own day and night (but no moon of its own). It has fourteen consecutive days of light, then fourteen consecutive days of darkness at any one place on its surface.

On a summer night in Phoenicia, New York, I often pause before going into the cabin to glance up at the heavens. I wonder then why others don't. Our nature seems to require that we look to the ground and not to the sky. I pause and crane my neck. Something blinks—a jetliner or a sputnik. Once in a while I witness a shooting star—something exploding in the heavens —and I marvel and feel lucky to be alive and have two feet planted on soil that revolves through space. I hate all science fiction, all made-up accounts of what will never be. It will surely be greater than what we imagine. I looked up at these same stars back in Tennessee when no man-made contraptions sped above. (It was kind of an event to spot a propellor-driven plane in the daytime.) And now—that one moment before I step into the upstate cabin—I take a wonderful, God-given pee, gazing above as I splatter below. There is no sound save crickets and the brook and my own stream. A billion galaxies and a billion stars in each of them up there! Are we all going there? Is Nelson Rockefeller up there already—and Tallulah Bankhead? We don't want to keep looking up there undoubtedly because we might cease to care what faced us straight ahead the next day down here. What does a Con Ed bill matter in the light of such stars? What does the wiles of a Henry Kissinger matter in the face of a billion twinkling, faraway lights?

There are those who earn their living at night, who honorably plow through the moonlit hours. They don't have the seniority necessary for the day shift; they can't find another job. Others are owls sentenced by their own bodies to nights and can only fall asleep at dawn. There are jazz musicians and bartenders and ladies of the evening, the gamblers and the sharks. There are criminals and madmen and prowlers of the street. There are those who slice into part of the dark night—the TV and radio performers who rise at 3 A.M. to be before camera and mike by six. The swing-shifters are dropped off dazed into the night, job completed, at midnight or 2 A.M. There are those who bed down but never know when they may have to clamor into the darkness, who sleep on the edge: the intern at the emergency room, the fireman, the man who runs a twenty-four-hour wrecker service. The bell rings and they jump into their pants. Lots of writers love the night. Balzac did. You draw the drapes, swill the coffee and scribble away. No interruptions, just your thoughts. The night is a frontier and it is a graveyard. Plants do not grow at night except by artificial light. The sun is what truly warms and nourishes and renews life. Night is when you die or lay low; it is what you are forced into from a secure, seemingly permanent base when you least expect it. It is when you face the worst.

But the sun also rises—as Hemingway pointed out from Ecclesiastes. . . . I am driving a green 1951 Plymouth Cambridge sedan down curvy, blacktopped 11E to Knoxville to watch the New York Giants play a spring exhibition game. My father sits beside me. A wonderful country scent wafts in through the open windows. The sun has burned off the morning dew and now its rays flood the countryside and glint off the car's chrome and paint I had so devotedly polished. Not a cloud in the blue sky. Green plants are shooting forth from the plowed fields beside us. I go fifty because of the curves. There are no speed limits, no interstates. We pass through Morristown, Bulls Gap and Jefferson City, right through the heart of those places, and each brings back memories to my father. He makes a comment or two but is mostly silent. He never says anything he doesn't feel like saying. I don't give those places a second thought, because they are as familiar to me as the palm of my hand. I dream of New York and California and far horizons.

My dad and I sit down close near home plate, and the sun is over our heads. We have got there early because my dad did not want to miss one second of watching the Giants. We were there before batting practice even started, among the first few souls in the park. He has been a fan since the days of John McGraw. He can quote batting and pitching statistics for hours and readily quotes remarks from McGraw and Christy Mathewson and a host of other Giants. He is loyal. He hasn't followed, or liked, another team since he was a boy. Today he catches a few beers by a concession stand. He will not drink beer in the stands, as he will not smoke a cigarette at an eating table. He was brought up that way. He is in his rolled-up shirtsleeves, and his hands are square and still quite strong. There is no jar he can't open or rock he can't lift. He puts away a beer in five or six long, hard pulls, the gurgles jumping in the bottle. Back to his beloved Giants.

They wear gray uniforms with bright blue piping and lettering, brand-new and neat and not a speck of grime on them. They laugh, those Giants. Leo Durocher struts by in his cocky way, the world in his palm, a grin and a wave to the stands. How those Giants swat the ball in batting practice, sending a white dot sizzling high into the deep blue sky. An outfielder throws up a glistening brown glove and snaps it in. They wear black spiked shoes unmarked now by dust. Their leg stockings fit snugly. Bobby Thomson swings and Monte Irvin does too, two powerful men—and here comes a rookie they have high hopes for, Willie Mays. Durocher is very solicitous of him, I notice. My dad is very keen on him, too. The game is played, and I forget who is on the other side or who wins. It doesn't matter. This is before the regular season begins—before it's all for real.

We drive back in midafternoon, the sun lower but still strong. In the glaring light, the radio plays country music, our cigarette smoke moves lazily for a while in the car and then rushes out the open windows. We are separated by time and age and our places in life, but we share jokes and a familiarity we don't find with others. How sweet the country air is, even through the fog of cigarette smoke. Biscuits and fried chicken and fat-backed beans wait for us at home. Maybe I'll have time to shoot a game of pool before supper and touch base with all my buddies. Night is a long way off.